WHEN CHURCH KIDS GO BAD

HOW TO LOVE AND WORK WITH RUDE, OBNOXIOUS, AND APATHETIC STUDENTS

LES CHRISTIE

 ZONDERVAN®

ZONDERVAN.com/
AUTHORTRACKER
follow your favorite authors

 youth
specialties

When Church Kids Go Bad: How to Work with and Love Rude, Obnoxious, and Apathetic Students
Copyright 2008 by Les Christie

Formerly titled: *When You Have to Draw the Line: Positive Discipline and How to Work with Rude, Obnoxious, and Apathetic Kids.*

Youth Specialties resources, 300 S. Pierce St., El Cajon, CA 92020 are published by Zondervan, 5300 Patterson Ave. SE, Grand Rapids, MI 49530.

Library of Congress Cataloging-in-Publication Data

Christie, Les John.
  When church kids go bad : how to work with and love rude, obnoxious, and apathetic students / by Les Christie.
    p. cm.
  Rev. ed.: When you have to draw the line. Ill. : Victor Books, c1988.
  Includes bibliographical references.
  ISBN 978-0-310-27665-4 (pbk.)
  1. Church work with teenagers. I. Christie, Les John. When you have to draw the line. II. Title.
  BV4447.C483 2008
  259'.23—dc22

                                                              2008027440

Cover design by SharpSeven Design
Interior design by Brandi K. Etheredge

Printed in the United States of America

---

08 09 10 11 12 • 20 19 18 17 16 15 14 13 12 11 10 9 8 7 6 5 4 3 2

Acknowledgments

I am so grateful to Jay Howver of Youth Specialties, who saw the potential for this book from the very beginning. Jay and I met at a restaurant to talk about the book during a YS convention. (I always like to meet Jay at a restaurant because he knows wonderful places to eat, he picks up the tab, and, oh yeah, he's also great company.) At that restaurant meeting was another friend, David Welch, a marketing poobah and a thought-provoking fellow. David also encouraged me to make this book to be part of the YS/Zondervan lineup.

Thanks to Jen Howver of VOD Communications, who suggested the clever title for the book.

A big thank-you goes out to my friend Emily Darlington, the faculty projects coordinator at William Jessup University, who typed the original manuscript. I am also grateful to her assistant, Torben Seikowsky.

A huge thank-you must go to Doug Davidson, my editor, for his attention not only to the overall picture of the book but also to its details. He was wonderful to work with and walked me through the editing process with warmth and kindness. His insights and observations made this a much better book. I am so grateful for his help in organizing and structuring the book and for his sensitivity to those who will be reading it.

Thanks to Roni Meek, who cocoordinated all the details of producing the book. She kept me in the loop in each stage of development.

Thanks to Mindi Godfrey, Zondervan's marketing and partnership coordinator, as well as to Karen Campbell and Leslie Lutes, who are all getting the word out about this book.

Special thanks to Holly Sharp for her creative ideas about the cover of the book, and to Brandi Etheredge for her fine work on the interior layout. And thank you to Heather Haggerty and Rich Cairnes for their close attention to detail as proofreaders.

Contents

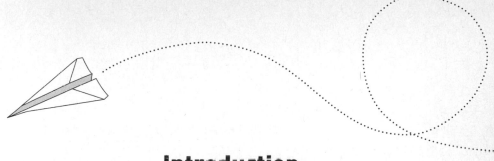

Introduction

I'll never forget the Sunday school class I was part of as a fourth-grader. I attended that church for only six months, and I didn't become a Christian until years later; yet my experience there was one of the reasons I wrote this book. My brief stint in that church taught me a lot about the effects of inadequate discipline.

The class contained about 14 fourth- to sixth-graders, over whom our teacher had absolutely no control. Each week featured a different form of chaos. Bibles and other materials were thrown around the room. Students entertained one another with obscene sounds and gestures. It was fun for about 10 minutes—until some of us smaller kids began to fear bodily damage from some of the larger students.

I can imagine how frustrated that poor teacher must have been. She was baffled about what to do with her unruly group. At the end of her rope and in absolute despair, she would often let us out of class early. She may have cared about us (she did remember to send us birthday cards); however, she could never remember our names in class and often seemed completely unprepared to teach. This only made it more difficult to keep our extremely active class under control.

I did have one positive experience with this church, but it came outside the Sunday school classroom. During the six months I attended, my parents would drop me off and pick me up in front of the church each Sunday. There was a woman who stood out front greeting people. She always called me by name and told me how glad she was that I was there. Each Sunday as I got into my parents' car, she said good-bye to me and invited me back next week. She had a wonderful smile and made me feel extremely welcome.

One particular Sunday, I was leaning against the church wall, watching the youth minister play ball with some high schoolers, when that friendly woman came up to me. I think she sensed my admiration of the youth minister, because she casually asked if I thought the youth minister was a sharp person. I was fairly shy at the time. I looked down and kicked the ground with my shoe and quietly said, "Yeah." Then she said something I'll always remember. She said, "You know, Les, I think you'd make a good youth minister someday!" That was the end of the conversation. My parents arrived, I got into the car, and they took me home. But I never forgot her words.

One reason I'm a youth minister today is because a woman whose name I don't even know believed I could do it. That incident taught me about the enormous influence adults can have on young people's lives through positive relationships. Today, every time I see a young person, I want to say something to encourage him or her, because I can never predict the impact of those words. And that's why this book will emphasize the importance of positive discipline when working with kids who can be rude, obnoxious, and apathetic.

There are thousands of books, pamphlets, and articles on the subject of discipline. Most of them are built around a single method of disciplining young people. But there's a big problem with any single-system approach to discipline. As Elizabeth Crisci described in her 1981 book *What Do You Do with Joe?* your average youth group might include Bashful Brooke, Turned-Off Tiffany, Know-It-All Nathan, Doubting Debra, Rebellious Ryan, Silly Sarah, Daydreaming Danielle, Troubled Tony, Friendless Fran, Unloved Lindsey, Slow-Learner Steven, Domineering Dana, Resentful Roger, and Super-Spiritual Scott. I would update Crisci's list for the 21st century by adding All-about-Appearance Allison, Computer-Geek Garrett, Incessant-Talker Isabella, Blue-Flame Brian, Substance-Abusing Samantha, Queen-Bee Quinn, Goth Gabrielle, Wannabe Wyatt, Starbucks-Addicted Sophia, Moody Mackenzie, Redneck Ray, Loud Lauren, Artsy Anthony, Whiner Will, Gang-Member Gavin, Snobby Savannah, and Class-Clown Connor.

No single approach will work at all times with all of these students. Each young person is unique. When it comes to the young people who are causing problems, some of them will cry if you so much as look at them crossly. There are others you suspect wouldn't budge even if you whacked them with a steel girder.

Disciplining kids is a hot issue for those of us who work with youth. The concerns come at us from every direction. Our pastors tell us some of "our kids" are disrupting the worship services. Teachers and other leaders resign because of the kids' behavior. We get aggravated ourselves when we try to present a creative program, only to watch the group come completely unglued. How can we keep disruptive kids and discipline problems from dominating our youth ministries?

It's my hope that *When Church Kids Go Bad* will offer you a wide range of practical and helpful ways to guide the young people in your group. Among the variety of strategies given, I am confident you'll find several that suit your style of youth ministry and the kids with whom you work.

Keep in mind that any new discipline method is bound to feel strange at first. When you attempt a new technique mentioned in *When Church Kids Go Bad*, be sure to give it an honest try and take enough time to understand and feel comfortable with it. If after sincere effort, you find that some recommended method feels foreign and just "isn't you," drop it and use another method.

Nearly every other book I've read on discipline has been focused on the preadolescent. Occasionally, I find a book with a token chapter aimed at the teen years, but most of these books assume that by the time kids are teenagers, they are unmovable, unchangeable, and unbendable. *When Church Kids Go Bad* is designed specifically for those of us working with junior and senior highers. I strongly believe students are still pliable and moldable at this age. As time moves on, behavior may become set in concrete—but during the teen years, we are still working with wet cement.

Howard Hendricks translates Ephesians 6:4: "But bring them up in *chastening* and *instruction* of the Lord." Hendricks says every competent physician practices two forms of medicine—corrective (chastening) medicine and preventive (instructive) medicine. In the same way, every good youth leader needs to practice both corrective and preventive forms of discipline. Unfortunately, many of us define *discipline* only in the corrective sense. *When Church Kids Go Bad* is intended not only to help you correct present discipline problems, but also to help you prevent future problems from occurring.

Remember that using the "D word" with your students doesn't mean you have to come down hard on them all the time. Focusing on discipline is not an excuse to take out your frustrations on disruptive class members. Instead, discipline is a tool to keep your group situations from disintegrating into the kind of chaos and confusion that is just as upsetting to students as it is to leaders. Positive discipline helps provide a learning environment that's both positive and safe—an environment to which your young people will want to return.

"This is our son, Shawn. We'll pick him up when he turns eighteen."

Why Do Kids Act That Way?

It's not easy being an adult youth leader or a parent today. You've heard that tune before, right? Parenting and youth ministry are tough jobs—and it's been that way for a long time. As rough as it is for today's parents and youth workers, we are just taking part in a long tradition passed down through the ages. Consider these not-so-modern examples:

> An angry father asks his teenage son, "Where did you go?" The boy, as he is trying to sneak home late at night says, "Nowhere." "Grow up," his father chides him. "Stop hanging around the public square and wandering up and down the street. Go to school. Night and day you torture me. Night and day you waste your time having fun." (Translated from 4,000-year-old Sumerian clay tablets)

> I see no hope for the future of our people if they are dependent on the frivolous youth of today. For certainly all youth are reckless beyond words. When I was a boy we were taught to be discreet and respectful of elders, but the present youth are exceedingly wild and impatient. (Ancient Greek poet Hesiod)

> Youth today love luxury. They have bad manners, contempt for authority, no respect for older people, and talk nonsense when they should work. Young people do not stand up any longer when adults enter the room. They contradict their parents, talk too much in company, guzzle their food, lay their legs on the table, and tyrannize their elders. (Socrates)

The world is passing through troublous times. The young people of today think of nothing but themselves. They have no reverence for parents or old age. They are impatient of all restraint. They talk as if they knew everything, and what passes for wisdom with us is foolishness with them. As for the girls, they are forward and immodest, and unwomanly in speech, behavior, and dress. (Peter the Hermit, 1274)

Our earth is degenerate—children no longer obey their parents. (Carved on stone 6,000 years ago by an Egyptian priest)

From there Elisha went up to Bethel. As he was walking along the road, some boys came out of the town and jeered at him. "Get out of here, baldy!" they said. "Get out of here, baldy!" (2 Kings 2:23, 9th century BC)

© 2004 Bob Schochet

*"The trouble with you kids these days is that you're spoiled.
Everything is made too easy for you. In my day we really had it rough!"*

Since the beginning of time, every generation of adults has said the present generation of young people is so much worse than their own generation. We adults have a tendency to idealize the past.

Now, you may be thinking, "Well, maybe those adults in the distant past might have idealized their teenage years—but I really was a much kinder, gentler, more compassionate, and better-behaved teen than most kids today." I know that feeling. I felt that way until a couple of years ago when I watched a rerun of an old *Dragnet* episode from the 1960s—back when I was a teenager. *Dragnet* was one of the first cop series on television. In this episode called "The Grenade," the two stars of the program, police officers Joe Friday and Bill Gannon, were talking in their squad car about the teenagers of my generation. I had to laugh as I listened to them repeating the same kind of comments I so often hear in reference to today's young people: "Kids have too much to say these days," "Kids today have lost any semblance of respect," "Why can't kids just be kids?" "It was never like this when we were kids."

I have a sign in my office that reads, "The older I get, the better I was." As adults we repress the memories of our early adolescent feelings and experiences. We forget what it was really like to be a 14-year-old. I think this faulty memory is a gift from God. He puts a software program in our brains that engages when we turn 20, and it erases our memories of all the stupid things we said, did, and thought during adolescence. This may be a pleasant place to be emotionally, but it's not an accurate view of how it really was "back when we were kids." The best parents and youth leaders are those who have an accurate memory of their own teen years.

The Struggle to Fit In

The next time you gather with some close friends for dinner, try playing the "Remember When?" game. Ask your friends to remember when they were adolescents. Do they remember someone making a remark about their appearance (the shape of his head, the size of her nose)? How did such remarks affect them? You will be amazed at the vivid memories most adults have of feeling criticized or rejected as teenagers. It's an important reminder of how sensitive teenagers are to criticism and rejection. They want to be accepted and liked, just as you did.

Not long ago, I played the "Remember When?" game with a few friends. Sitting back in a comfortable easy chair, Sharon remembered a name she was called in junior high. She has a bright-red birthmark on her upper lip, and the other kids called her "dog face" and would yell things like, "Here doggy, here doggy." She found it extremely difficult to cope—so difficult she had contemplated suicide. Mark talked about how shy he was in his teen years, remembering how his mother used to answer any questions directed at him before he could get an answer out. John remembered feeling insecure about his body and never wanting to take a shower in the school's public shower stalls after physical education class during junior high. He recalled how most of the students would just run through the showers and grab a towel.

I remember the fear that gripped me during a youth meeting following my junior year of high school, right after I had become a Christian. Our church youth group had a prayer circle in which everyone held hands and prayed aloud. I had never prayed in public, and as it got closer to my turn, I was so nervous I started to perspire and shake. When it came my turn, I said something quickly (I have no idea what I prayed) and the prayer time moved on to the next person. To this day I remember my intense fear of being embarrassed in front of my peers.

It's easy to forget or minimize the intense trials and tribulations many young people go through during junior high and high school. I recently read a newspaper story about a boy in a small high school whom other students made fun of because he was overweight. They called him "blimp" and "fatso" and "lard," and made him the butt of every joke. He was a nice kid who never gave his teachers any trouble—but one day he finally broke. He brought a gun to school and shot several students, and finally turned the gun on himself. His suicide note explained he could no longer endure the ridicule.

The Teenage Emotional and Physical Roller Coaster

Emotionally, young people are on a roller coaster. It's either Death Valley or Mount Everest. You've probably experienced this as a youth leader. One week, your youth group meeting is fantastic—students are well behaved, listening intently, and asking terrific questions. You go out of the meeting riding on a cloud—life is tremendous, your ministry is a great success, and you love kids. But the next week it's a disaster. You wonder if they went home the previous week and called one another, saying, "Hey, we were too nice tonight. Let's be sure and make some trouble next week." During those times, we may feel like all our teaching just goes in one ear and out the other. It can be horribly frustrating.

Adolescence is a period of transition, a period of change—and a prevailing characteristic of change is instability. We see this in the fast, intense, and ever-changing emotional world of many teens. Even a relatively small stimulus will sometimes trigger a more intense reaction. Dr. G. Keith Olson describes the variety of intense emotions a teenage girl might experience over a brief period one morning :

6:30: Jennifer wakes up reluctantly, dreading this day that she is absolutely positive will be awful.

6:50: Jen is elated because she can still fit into her favorite pair of pants.

7:00: She is upset because her hair will not do what she wants it to do. She knows she will feel humiliated when other kids see her.

7:30: She is both thrilled and apprehensive because Jeff called, asking to drive her to school that day.

7:50: Jen has a feeling of pride, even arrogance, as her friends see her driving into the school parking lot, snuggled close to Jeff.

7:55: She feels indignant and angry when a friend walks off to class ahead of her after making a snippy remark about her special transportation.

Over the course of just 90 minutes Jennifer has experienced intense feelings of reluctance, dread, elation, humiliation, thrill, apprehension, pride, arrogance, indignation, and anger. And while cultural and social influence may cause girls to be more expressive than boys about experiencing these intense feelings, we can be sure that guys go through many of the same ups and downs.

Romantic problems are often a big part of the roller coaster many teens are riding. The girl whose boyfriend dumped her or the boy who was turned down one too many times by the girl of his dreams is likely to be moody and depressed, show no interest in church or youth group, and be obsessed with thoughts of lost opportunities for romance.

The differences we experience from week to week with our students' behavior also have a lot to do with the tremendous physical changes adolescents are experiencing. Adolescents are always worrying about something:

- Teens worry they are growing too rapidly, too slowly, or too unevenly.
- Teens worry they are developing too much, too little, or in the wrong places.
- Teens worry about their height, their weight, and the condition of their skin.
- Teens worry that during a long kiss they'll have to breathe through their nose and their nose will be stopped up.
- Teens worry that there is a right way to kiss and they don't know it.
- Teens worry that their dates will able to tell they don't know.
- Teen girls worry that their breasts are too round or point in different directions.
- Teen boys worry that they will get breasts.
- Teen boys worry that they will never be able to grow a mustache.
- Teen girls worry that they will grow a mustache.

Adolescents sometimes feel their bodies are conspiring against them. But the big physical changes happening in adolescence aren't just the ones that involve those pesky hormones, hair, and pimples. In recent years, neuroscientists like Dr. Jay Giedd at the National Institutes of Health have found that the adolescent brain undergoes a massive remodeling of its basic structure, in areas that affect everything from logic and language to impulses and intuition. (*The Primal Teen* by Barbara Strauch, p. 13.) We now know the brain continues to change and is not completely formed until the mid-20s. (My wife often jokes that the process seems to take an additional 20 years for most men!) The point is that God is not finished with these adolescent brains.

So much of the hurt and pain in young people between ages 12 and 20 stems from a hopelessness that comes from believing they are inferior. It's that awful feeling that nobody likes them; that they're not as good as others; that they're failures, losers, or personal disasters; that they're ugly, or unintelligent, or don't have as much ability as someone else. It's that depressing feeling of worthlessness. Teenage boys especially tend to strike out physically at others when they feel powerless to get their way by other means. These young people often lack verbal skills and believe in a distorted version of the actions-speak-louder-than-words model of living. Understanding the physical and emotional changes teenagers are going through will help you understand their behavior and extreme mood swings.

How Things Have Changed

As I've said, I don't think kids today are all that different from those of previous generations. Since the beginning of civilization, kids have needed the same things—to feel loved, wanted, secure, safe, and cared for. The changes in body and brain functioning, the huge emotional ups and downs, and the deep desire to fit in—these challenges of adolescence are anything but unique to this generation of young people.

© 1984 Rob Suggs

On the other hand, I think the world that kids are growing up in today is dramatically different than the one faced by previous generations. One of the biggest changes is the way violence (and the threat of violence) shapes the lives of so many young people.

A third-grade girl in New Orleans recently took a .357 Magnum to school to protect her from a boy who was allegedly harassing her. Margaret Ensley's 17-year-old son Michael caught a bullet in the hallway of his high school in Reseda, California. (She says a teen shot her son because he thought Michael gave him a funny look.) On the streets of many cities, girls carry small guns in their purses and razor blades in their mouths in case they need to protect themselves, or find a victim ripe for the taking. Law enforcement and public health officials describe a virtual epidemic of youth violence in recent years. "We're talking about younger and younger kids committing more and more serious crimes," says Indianapolis prosecuting attorney Jeff Modsett. "Violence is becoming a way of life."

Between 1987 and 1994, the number of teenagers arrested for murder around the country increased by an astounding 85 percent, according to the Department of Justice. The good news is that by 2003, the percentage had dropped to the 1987 level. However, children from the ages of 10 to 17 now account for 17 percent of all violent crime arrests. Teenagers are not just the perpetrators—they are also the victims. A 2005 survey done by the Uhlich Children's Advantage Network (UCAN), a multiservice agency for at-risk children and their families in Chicago, concluded that 39 percent of teens fear being shot sometime in their life. An estimated 100,000 students carry a gun to school, according to the National Education Association. The Justice Department estimates that each year, nearly one million young people between the ages of 12 and 19 are raped, robbed, or assaulted—often by their peers.

John Taylor Gatto, who was the New York State Teacher of the Year in 1991, offers this sad commentary on the world young people are struggling to fit into: "I've come slowly to understand what it is I really teach: a curriculum of confusion, class position, arbitrary justice, vulgarity, rudeness, and disrespect for privacy. I teach how to fit into a world I don't want to live in."

The Information Age

Young people once learned how to live by being mentored by their elders. I can remember stories of my great-great-grandfather over in England who at the age of 14 went to live with a master carpenter's family until age 21. During those years he learned the trade of carpentry. It was the only way to learn it.

Changes in technology have dramatically transformed the way information is passed from generation to generation. It began with the development and later popularization of the printing press, which eventually made books and the printed page a primary source for the transfer of knowledge.

With the invention of the television, information technology was further transformed, as televised images became available to the masses and changed the values and lifestyles of teens all around the world. TV commercials teach kids that material goods are what make life worthwhile and that every problem can be solved in 30 seconds. Television also does not always show a fair and or accurate portrayal of life and especially elders—often portraying parents and church leaders as idiots who are out of touch with the world. Just compare the attitude toward parenting and families in TV series from the 1960s like *Leave It to Beaver* or *Father Knows Best* with the depictions in more recent shows such as *The Simpsons, Two and a Half Men,* or *The Osbournes.*

The personal computer and the Internet have caused an even more dramatic change in how knowledge is passed on. Teenagers pick up computer skills quite easily but many older people find it much harder. Don Tapscott in his book *Growing Up Digital,* asks:

> What makes this generation different from all others before it? It is the first to grow up surrounded by digital media... Today's kids are so bathed in bits that they think it's all part

of the natural landscape. To them, the digital technology is no more intimidating than a toaster. For the first time in history, children are more comfortable, knowledgeable, and literate than their parents about an innovation central to society.

When Everything Nailed Down Is Coming Loose

In today's youth culture, there are no absolutes. Young people are bombarded with the idea that there is no right or wrong. This piles confusion on confusion, as nothing in life seems secure for a teen.

The disappearance of marriage as a dependable, permanent structure has caused many changes in families. Many parents are going through their own midlife crises. Self-absorbed with their own problems (divorce, job changes, unfilled goals), they cannot protect, guide, or support their teenagers.

Families are also smaller, and those smaller families are more mobile (20 percent of the population moves every year). The kids in smaller families tend to be more self-centered because parents are able to cater to the individual needs of their kids.

Kids who grew up in families where there is child abuse and maltreatment, spouse abuse, and a history of violent behavior learn early on to lash out physically when they are frustrated or upset. Poverty exacerbates the situation. Parents who haven't finished high school, who are unemployed or on welfare, or who began their families when they were teenagers are more likely to have delinquent teens.

Thousands of kids feel as if they are constantly in a pressure cooker. And while most teenagers seem to handle pressure fairly well, adult youth leaders still need to know the causes of stress and how to help teenagers deal with it. The stress teenagers face frequently mirrors adult stress. Teenage concerns about their grades in school or relationship troubles with a boyfriend or girlfriend are similar to the job or marital concerns adults face. And many teenagers also face the stress of breakdown in their own family life. *U.S. News and World Report* reported on a federal government study showing growing psychological stress on children and adolescents. The study stated, "In the last fifteen years, 15.6 million marriages have ended in divorce, disrupting the lives of 16.3 million children under the age of eighteen."

Dr. Howard Hendricks in *Heaven Help the Home* puts it this way:

> We are living in a generation in which everything nailed down is coming loose. The things that people once said could not happen are happening. And thoughtful, though often unregenerate, individuals are asking, "Where is the glue with which to reassemble the disintegrating and disarrayed parts?

Where Do You Fit In?

I firmly believe that adult youth leaders can help provide some of the "glue" that is lacking in the lives of many young people today. But that's unlikely to happen if our youth groups mirror the disintegration and disarray students experience in so much of their lives.

If we want to create settings for youth that will help them grow into Christian maturity, I believe it's helpful to start by considering our own attitudes toward discipline. Which of the following disciplinarians is most similar to you?

- Buddy the Permissive: Buddy avoids absolutes and places no demands on his kids. His philosophy is that kids are basically good, and he refuses to be negative with them. He likes to let group members find their own way and feels his role is not to control or correct, but to support and encourage.
- Beth the Benevolent: Beth shows deep respect for and sensitivity to each individual in her group. She feels discipline is not for her but for the good of the students. She looks for long-range results rather than temporary solutions, and remains aware of her own sinfulness and shortcomings.
- Rocky the Authoritarian: Rocky believes he has the final word in all disputes. His authority cannot be questioned. He places unrealistic demands on students and makes no allowances or exceptions. He

feels his duty is to control, and he's not above using sarcasm and put-downs. He sees fear and intimidation as the best way to achieve discipline results.

Draw an "X" on the spot on the continuum where you think you are now:

Permissive---------------------Benevolent---------------------Authoritarian

Naturally, Beth the Benevolent might sound like the person whose discipline style is most balanced and modeled on Christlike behavior—so we may be tempted to say we're like her. But if we're honest, most of us would probably admit we lean toward one end of the line or the other. Sometimes we even jump from one extreme to the other!

Now think about where you would like to be on the scale above. The good news is that you can develop an effective style of discipline that can become an important ministry tool—a tool that will not only help the kids you work with and care about but also might save your sanity! Developing that kind of effective discipline style is exactly what this book is all about.

In *When Church Kids Go Bad*, we'll look at how you can prevent discipline problems or at least put a stop to them before they become huge. We'll think together about where we want students to be when they leave our care, and how we can help them get there. We'll look at some ways to keep kids on your side even when disciplining them. We'll dig into specific methods for handling difficult kids and we'll tackle the everyday problems you face as an adult youth leader. We'll even consider the challenges of ministering among high-risk kids. My hope is that this book will leave you feeling prepared, confident, and even more in love with the students God has placed in your care.

Now Ask Yourself

1. Think of the discipline problems that were prevalent in your teen years and compare and contrast them with the discipline problems faced by teachers and youth leaders today.

2. What types of discipline problems are in your city at home/school/church?

3. How are we doing in the three areas above in regard to counteracting these types of behavior?

4. What were your feelings when you read about the teacher with 13 years' teaching experience? Do you agree with his assessment? Why?

5. What kind of kids do you find toughest to love? *(Read through the list below and circle three or four types of kids you personally find hardest to love.)*

The Pastor's Kids	New Kids	Smelly Kids
Questioning Kids	My Own Kids	Cool Kids
Middle School Boys	Rural Kids	Pranksters
Middle School Girls	Urban Kids	Preps
Moody Kids	Christian School Kids	Whiners
Athletes	Homeschooled Kids	Kids Who Don't Listen
Mathletes	Misbehaving Kids	Gossips
Goth Kids	Loud Kids	Bullies
AD/HD Kids	Hurt Kids	The Class Clown
Unattractive Kids	Know-It-Alls	Incessant Talkers
Shy Kids	Band Geeks	Bible Nerds
Nerds	Groupies	Computer Geeks
Artists	Rich Kids	Freshmen
Cheerleaders	Attractive Kids	Seniors

Discipline: The Goal Is Maturity

Karen was the youth group "kiss-up." She was always polite and well behaved when the youth leaders were looking in her direction, but when the adults' backs were turned, she could be a terror. Confronting Karen about her rude and obnoxious behavior was difficult because she thought she was hiding it from all the authority figures in her life (parents, teachers, pastors, youth leaders). But she wasn't. Karen's life was always in turmoil. She had to be the center of attention in every activity, and her emotions were extremely volatile—either incredibly happy or in the pits. She always had a dramatic story to tell that could not wait.

I wish I could say Karen's values were changed by her involvement in the church youth group. But the truth is that she just learned to fine-tune and perfect her hypocrisy. She never learned how to be comfortable with herself and take responsibility for her own behavior. On a first meeting, she appeared to be a wonderful example of what a Christian environment can do for a young person's life. But those who really knew Karen were aware she was just going through the outward motions of being a Christian without internalizing those values.

Kids like Karen remind us that the ultimate goal of our discipline isn't to get kids to behave at youth group or whenever adults are watching. Our goal is to help kids grow into Christian maturity and encourage self-discipline. Our objective is to prepare young people to make their own decisions in life and discipline themselves. We want to prepare each young person to become a fully functioning, mature Christian adult.

Discipline may be defined as "training that develops inner self-control in which values are internalized." The discipline we offer should help teenagers establish values and principles they can use to conduct their lives—even when the adult youth leaders aren't watching. Our major emphasis must be on getting students to grow, mature, and learn responsibility for their own behavior.

It may be possible to use bribery, force, cleverness, and peer pressure to make young people do what we say. But who wants a youth group full of robots who are merely going through the motions? Such students will never grow into mature Christians who make their own decisions in life. We can't assume our discipline efforts are successful simply because young people are compliant. That compliance may mean changing behavior only in the presence of authority. In street language, it's called "cheesing"—telling us what we want to hear. But a cheese ball is mostly air—it's not what it appears to be. It's not the real thing.

I'm reminded of the mother who kept asking her five-year-old daughter to sit down. After asking repeatedly, the frustrated mother finally forcibly placed the young girl in the chair, insisting, "You *will* sit down!" The little girl merely smiled. When the mother asked why she was smiling, the girl replied, "I may be sitting down on the outside, but inside I'm standing up." Simply getting young people to go through the motions of obedience does not accomplish our real goal.

Several years ago I went to Sea World in San Diego. Outside a small amphitheater was a sign that said "Roller-Skating Ducks." My curiosity was aroused, so I went in and took a seat. Sure enough, the music started and out came these little ducks with tiny roller skates taped to their webbed feet. They were roller-skating to the music. But I could tell their hearts weren't into it!

We can do the same thing with kids. We can get them to do a variety of things—even things they really don't want to do. But on the inside nothing has changed. You can tell their hearts just aren't in it.

What's My Motivation?

When an outside force causes us to take action, that's called external, or extrinsic, motivation. It is the promise of reward or the threat of punishment that makes the individual respond. The problem is that a person motivated by threats or rewards may never internalize the behavior and become self-disciplined. The acid test for a person in authority is: What are your people like when you aren't there? You may win the daily battle but not necessarily the war, if your constant presence is needed to ensure proper behavior.

Leonard Berkowitz, in *The Development of Motives and Values in the Child*, describes how a young person internalizes values:

> When he is very young, of course, the child must be controlled by direct parental action. The mother must prevent her child from touching the hot stove...As he gets older, he learns that his parents want him to do certain things at certain times and not to do other things. He gets approval for carrying out the desired actions and some form of punishment if he departs from his parents' standards...This type of self-control is, however, ultimately based on the anticipation of detection; the child carries out the desired action or avoids the prohibited behavior because he believes that the people who can reward or punish him will find out what he has done. It is not until he has truly internalized parental and societal moral standards that he will behave in a socially proper fashion solely because that is the "right" thing.

What do you want your young people to be like when they grow up? Most of the parents and youth leaders I've met say they want to "influence" their young people to become responsible, independent adults. They want their kids to be able to make mature decisions about faith, work, marriage, and parenthood. They want them to be discriminating in their judgment of people and ideas, and to live fully with a sense of adventure, unafraid to explore the world (and even the universe) around them. They want their young people to be flexible enough to accept change, courageous enough to meet new challenges, and loving and sensitive enough to care deeply about life and people.

We need to help young people internalize the standards that will help them make these important decisions. One way to help them internalize these standards is to ask them to think about how they would like things to be. Too often students only react to what their youth leaders tell them to do, rather than being helped to decide what they would like to do for themselves. You can help students learn to make decisions by asking questions. You can ask them to list the pros and cons of the action they are contemplating. What are the ramifications and consequences of that decision? What other alternatives are available? You may want to show students how you make decisions in life. How do you determine what kind of car to purchase? If you're married, how do you and your spouse decide whose family you'll visit on Thanksgiving and Christmas? How do you budget your money? By helping young people think about the decisions they face, we help them develop discipline.

Discipline often gets bad press because it's misunderstood. Discipline is not about chaining young people to their seats or putting them in iron cages. People think discipline is synonymous with punishment, but in the Bible that's not the intended meaning at all. The word *discipline* comes from the same root as *disciple*. The root of the word *disciple* means "learner"; in both Hebrew and Greek, the words we translate *discipline* actually mean "training" or "education." So discipline involves instruction and training as well as correcting, and it is to be motivated by love and concern. (See Hebrews 12.)

Gordon MacDonald in *Parents and Teenagers* shares his definition of discipline:

> To me, discipline is the deliberate creation of stress in a relationship with your children in order to help them grow and learn. Discipline is setting them to a task to exercise, strengthen, and help them mature. Discipline is forcing them to face painful questions that need to be wrestled with. What a coach takes a team through before a contest is discipline.

With discipline you are making disciples of your young people. Disciples of a sport like tennis or running will alter their behavior, watch their diets, and change their daily schedules in noticeable ways. To be a responsible member of a youth group requires the same attentiveness.

Positive Discipline vs. Negative Discipline

Discipline that focuses primarily on punishment as a way to get a young person to behave properly is what's often called "negative discipline." A negative disciplinarian threatens, frightens, snarls, growls, bristles, and becomes just plain nasty in order to persuade young people to behave. Even if this kind of external pressure gets immediate results, when the pressure lets up, so does the person's response. Negative discipline usually backfires.

Negative discipline can destroy a young person's sense of being loved and wanted. It can leave him feeling insecure and worthless. Negative discipline implies getting even, retaliation, vengeance, and exacting a penalty. Of course, all these dangers are increased whenever negative discipline is cruel, unreasonably severe, or prolonged.

Guilt is another common motivator in negative discipline. But using guilt to get your teen to do something is destructive. Guilt is a tremendously difficult feeling to carry around inside. And even if your young person does change her behavior because she feels guilty, she will resent it; that resentment, coupled with feelings of guilt, can produce intense feelings of anger.

Negative discipline can help control some behavior by establishing an avoidance response. But negative discipline alone never teaches young people to be responsible, motivated, and cooperative. Any improved behavior due to negative discipline simply means the young person has realized that, in this situation, the cost of negative discipline outweighs the benefits of misbehaving. The young person may change the way she behaves, but not change the way she wants to behave.

I've heard that you can train fleas. Apparently, if you throw some fleas in a jar and put the lid back on, for a few minutes you will hear a popping noise. The fleas will jump from the bottom to the top, and their little bodies will crash against the lid for a few minutes. Eventually, they will get wise and won't jump as high—they'll jump to a height just beneath the lid. (After a while, even a flea realizes hitting its head on the lid isn't much fun). After a few hours of this, you can unscrew the lid, and the fleas won't jump out. They have the ability to jump higher than the top of the jar. But something tells them if they jump too high there will be pain. In the same way, negative discipline may make a teenager behave the way you want him or her to just to avoid pain. But inside, nothing has changed.

The problem with negative discipline is that it's effective only as long as the threat hangs over an individual's head. Negative discipline does not teach the long-term benefits of changing behavior. When the threat of negative discipline has been removed, people are likely to resume their inappropriate behavior again. Consider how people tend to drive when they know a police officer is sitting beside the freeway with a radar gun. As long as that police car is visible, most people will carefully stay within the speed limit. But some of those same people are willing to drive at unsafe speeds if the police aren't visible and they think they can get away with it. Negative discipline procedures make the adult youth leader a police officer in the youth group.

Negative discipline may curb some unacceptable behavior. But negative discipline in itself does not teach or motivate a young person toward more desirable behavior. It tells a young person what *not* to do—it doesn't tell him what to do. Consider our prison system. If punishment were effective in teaching people better behavior, then nearly anyone released from prison after several years of incarceration would go straight from then on. But a recent study showed that more than two-thirds of released prisoners were arrested again within three years. Of course, there are all kinds of reasons why someone who has been imprisoned is more likely to end up there again. But that doesn't change the basic fact that imprisonment merely keeps a person off the street for a period of time; it does very little to encourage rehabilitation or true changes in thinking and behavior.

On the other hand, positive discipline involves a combination of encouragement, consistency, fairness, and high expectations to train young people. A positive disciplinarian uses words, deeds, or circumstances to develop maturity in the young person—which is the ultimate goal of youth ministry. (See Colossians 1:28.) Our task is to prepare, disciple, and train young people to serve God with their lives, to bring them to maturity, wholeness, and completeness in Christ. Through positive discipline, we develop mature young people who know themselves, accept themselves, and control themselves.

Positive discipline is more an attitude and atmosphere than an action. It is a tool, not a weapon. It is an expression of love, not anger. Discipline in the true biblical sense is positive and encouraging—in fact, it's even proof of love. The remainder of this book is dedicated to helping you become a positive disciplinarian.

Dr. Bruce Narramore, in his excellent book *Help! I'm a Parent*, offers the following chart to differentiate between negative discipline and positive discipline:

	Negative Discipline	Positive Discipline
Outlook	Eye for an eye	Done *for* kid, not *to* kid
Purpose	To inflict penalty for an offense	To train for correction and maturity
Focus	Past misdeed or behavior	Future correct deeds
Attitude	Hostility and frustration	Love and concern
Resulting Emotion	Fear and guilt	Security

Too Little Discipline or Too Much?

Some adults believe it's a mistake to teach young people self-control. They believe it's best to stand back and allow teenagers to find their own paths and make their own mistakes, rather than offering them firm guidance. While I disagree with this type of thinking, I understand what motivates it. Young people need to express their independence, but our attempts to control and micromanage every moment of their lives really can make things worse. Too many rules and get-tough leaders offend kids and run them off.

However, the hands-off, anything-goes approach is equally disruptive. A teacher who has a *laissez-faire* approach loses kids. When the kids who've left the group are asked why, they often say they've stopped attending because the class was so wild and chaotic. Not all kids care for the loud, obnoxious behavior of their peers. Chaos might be fun for a few minutes, but not forever. Kids want order for the security and safety it gives them.

This hands-off style is common among adult youth leaders who fear they'll lose the kids' friendship if they react any other way. But the anything-goes approach carries a number of negative attributes. Think about what happens when a leader doesn't seem to notice or care about the disruptive noise from the group:

- It teaches kids it's okay to talk when someone else is speaking.
- It offends the kids who want to listen but can't because of the noise.
- It says: "This is competition. May the loudest or longest talker win."

If we want an environment that attracts kids and encourages good behavior, we have to fall somewhere between the two extremes. We're not called to be watchdogs, drill sergeants, or undercover cops, but we're not called to roll over and play dead, either. We don't need to be authoritarian, but we do have to be authoritative. We can't be permissive, but we have to be sensitive to everyone's needs. Kids need a comfortable environment free of excessive control, but some control must remain.

Some Dos and Don'ts of Discipline

Fair and reasonable discipline is like a fence that provides protection and defines limits, demonstrating both care and concern. Like a good fence, our discipline needs to be strong enough to do the job for which it was intended, but flexible enough to account for unexpected situations and different kinds of kids. (Don't forget that some young people require more discipline than others—that's just the way teens are.)

To be an effective youth leader / fence builder, here are a few "dos and don'ts" to keep in mind:

- Do make sure youth group members know where the fence is. Kids need to know where the boundaries are. As long as they stay within the defined boundaries, discipline is not necessary.
- Don't make your fence so wide that young people can do virtually anything they want and still be within the boundaries.
- Don't build the fence so tight that there is no room for the youth group members to breathe or so close that it stifles creativity. Trying to maintain a tight fence that is suffocating requires almost constant vigilance and often leads to constant discipline situations.
- Do make sure your fence boundaries are appropriate for the age and temperament of your group members. Limits should be redefined as young people mature.

I don't know of any young person who doesn't want to know where the boundaries are. There is security in knowing the limits. Young people don't want to have the boundaries hammered on the door of their youth room like Luther's 95 theses. They don't want to hear the rules recited every morning when they awaken. But they do want to know that there are rules and that they will be enforced.

Giving a young person complete freedom and license is recognized today for what it is—a grave mistake. It places too much responsibility on young shoulders that are not yet ready to carry that burden. The weight of responsibility can be crushing. But too much discipline can have a very similar effect, giving the young person a feeling of failure. Again, the burden is too heavy to bear.

Biblical Reasons for Discipline

Scripture has a lot to say about the need for discipline in the lives of young people. "Discipline your children," says Proverbs 29:17, "and they will give you peace." Although the focus in this and other passages tends to be more on the responsibilities of parents, I think the same principles apply for those of us who work with kids in youth ministry. Colossians 1:28 says we are called to help one another grow in Christian maturity: "We proclaim him, admonishing and teaching everyone with all wisdom, so that we may present everyone fully mature in Christ."

We see the importance of discipline in 1 Samuel 3:13 when the Lord speaks to Samuel about Eli, who was the high priest: "For I told him [Eli] that I would judge his family forever because of the sin he knew about; his sons blasphemed God, and he failed to restrain them." It's clear that what really ticked God off was not just the sin of Eli's sons, but also the fact that Eli did not discipline them.

But the foundational principle for an effective approach to discipline is unconditional love for the kids in our care. Just as God's fatherly love is characterized by tenderness and mercy so must our love for our students be. This love guides, corrects, and may even bring some pain at times: "No discipline seems pleasant at the time, but painful. Later on, however, it produces a harvest of righteousness and peace for those who have been trained by it" (Hebrews 12:11).

We see the centrality of love in both the teachings and actions of Jesus. Jesus likened himself to a loving shepherd who cares about the well-being of each of his sheep. In the gospel of John, Jesus gave his disciples a new commandment emphasizing the centrality of love: "As I have loved you, so you must love one another. By this everyone will know that you are my disciples, if you love one another" (John 13:34-35). Just a few verses later, we see that love doesn't mean Jesus was unwilling to confront his disciples, as he rebukes Peter for boasting about his willingness to die with Jesus (v. 38). Yet even though Peter goes on to deny Jesus three times (just as Jesus had predicted), the risen Christ reaches out to Peter with loving compassion, restoring him to the community (John 21:15-19).

Paul offers parents—and, by extension, youth workers—a warning about the subject of discipline: "Do not exasperate your children; instead, bring them up in the training and instruction of the Lord" (Ephesians 6:4). The King James Version uses these words: "Provoke not your children to wrath." So what kinds of things do we parents and youth leaders do that provoke and exasperate our young people? Sometimes we:

- compare or show favoritism
- accept young people only conditionally
- embarrass or ridicule
- ignore
- behave inconsistently
- show a lack of sensitivity
- fail to forgive
- have too few rules
- overreact
- use sarcasm
- assign tasks that are too difficult
- put kids down
- condescend
- discipline kids in front of their peers
- accuse falsely
- are impatient
- interrupt
- call kids names
- fail to respect privacy
- have too many rules
- punish unjustly
- shout or yell

Proverbs 17:9 is a good reminder for all of us in youth ministry: "Love forgets mistakes; nagging about them parts the best of friends" (TLB). We need to avoid the temptation to nag our students. By nagging, I mean reminding a kid of something even when we know he hasn't forgotten. Few things are less effective in promoting the behavior we desire. Nagging is as widespread as the common cold. "Don't talk so much. You keep putting your foot in your mouth. Be sensible and turn off the flow!" (Proverbs 10:19, TLB).

Now Ask Yourself

1. What are you doing in the area of discipline? Are your methods causing inner changes of behavior/values or just outward appearances of responsible behavior?

2. Describe what you want your young people to be like after they leave your youth group.

3. What kind of misbehavior tends to tick you off the most? Circle those behaviors you find most irritating from a discipline perspective:

- Bickering among group members
- Apathy
- Waiting to be entertained
- Lack of commitment or not taking God seriously
- Lack of respect for adults or others
- Arrogance
- Self-centeredness, cliques
- Unwillingness to listen
- Disrespect for rules and authority
- Cell phones ringing at inappropriate times
- Complaining, negative attitude
- Lying
- Vandalism
- Put-downs
- Acting too cool
- Know-it-alls
- Not listening
- Not cleaning up after a mess
- Horseplay
- Stubbornness
- Talking when someone else is talking
- Rudeness
- Bullying
- Belches
- Text messaging during meetings
- Listening constantly to music on electronic devices
- Kids pushing the limit
- Coming to meetings late
- iPods and other devices turned on during meetings
- Spilling food and stomping it into the carpet
- Spitting
- Expressions made in a whiny voice, such as—

"Who cares"

"Whatever"

"Stupid"

"I'm not doing that"

"I didn't know"

"My father's an elder, board member, council member, etc."

"All my friends do/don't"

"Make me"

4. What is the difference between positive discipline and negative discipline?

5. If discipline is like a fence, what kind of fence are you using? When is it too close (restrictive) or too far removed (permissive)?
   - Picket fence
   - Movable fence
   - Temporary fence
   - Electric fence
   - Chain-link fence
   - Barbed-wire fence
   - Brick wall
   - Door

6. Do you think 2 Timothy 3:2-5 describes today's generation of young people? Why or why not?

7. Describe the kind of discipline God uses with us.

8. Think of areas in your ministry where you have "provoked a young person to anger." Has this been cleared up?

9. How do you feel about taking verses directed to parents and applying them to youth leaders? Is there a fine line or danger in doing this? Are some adult youth leaders trying to take the place of parents?

© 1985 Doug Hall

"Then it's agreed. The theme for this year's youth convention is 'Hey, Gang! Let's Not Trash the Hotel!' "

3

Dealing with Problem Behavior

We talked in the very first chapter about some of the challenges adolescents face. Change is part of being a teenager—physical change, emotional change, and spiritual change. The massive and unsettling transitions kids experience during their teenage years can be a tremendous source of stress and confusion. And these changes can also be a primary cause for the kinds of behavior that keep many youth workers pulling out their own hair!

One of our primary challenges as youth leaders is to give teenagers concrete ways to deal with their stress. We cannot take away the potential pain and hurt that life sometimes brings—but we can teach teenagers positive ways to cope.

To be helpful to our young people, we need to respond genuinely to their moods and feelings without being caught up in them. We need to help our teenagers with their anger, fear, and confusion, without becoming angry, fearful, and confused ourselves. We need to be sensitive to their feelings without losing our perspective.

One of the problems with this is that young people often don't know how they feel. They are often experiencing feelings that are totally new to them, and they can't even begin to put these feelings into words. They are embarrassed and confused because they can't fully understand or express their feelings. Since they don't want to admit that inability to their adult youth leaders, kids may be reluctant to open up and confide in us.

One of the most important things we can do is to offer kids a consistent and caring presence as they walk through these difficult years. By spending time with students, by drawing them out and showing sensitivity to their feelings (whether the feelings are expressed or not), we can build the kind of strong relationships with young people that can help them find productive ways to deal with the feelings they are experiencing.

Keep in mind that drastic, lightning-quick changes in feelings and moods are both common and completely age appropriate for teens. These shifts are both normal and natural during adolescence. While adult youth leaders may still find these abrupt changes irritating, exasperating, and difficult to cope with, it may help to realize "this too shall pass."

Dramatic spiritual shifts are as common as emotional ones. Church youth groups are known for coming home from summer retreats or mission trips on a "spiritual high." Unfortunately, the spiritual valleys between these special events are equally common. This characteristic cycling between mountaintop highs and valley lows is usually not so much a sign of an unhealthy spirituality as a product of adolescent emotional changeability.

As we deal with students who are misbehaving, it's important to deal with teens on their level, and avoid statements that only widen the generational gap. In trying to connect with kids, adults often make the mistake of saying, "When I was your age…" This phrase brings instant deafness to young people. They do not want to hear about "ancient history"— especially if the point of our story is to show how good we were and how bad they are in comparison. Even if they hear us, they won't believe we were as hard working, sensible, smart, thrifty, and well behaved as we say. In fact, sometimes they have difficulty imagining the adults in their lives were ever young. Comparing ourselves with them—and making ourselves look better—will not encourage kids nor will it help them grow closer to us. Show kids that you understand their feelings and that you care—without the "when-I-was-your-age" speech.

It's easy to lose touch with what's going on with young people. So ask kids what kinds of pressure they experience, and then listen to what they say. The key word is *listen*. We can help alleviate some of the stress kids are feeling simply by being attentive and offering compassionate responses and ideas. Provide a safe environment for your group members to talk about their pressures by being available, by listening instead of lecturing, and by suggesting healthy ways to deal with stress.

"I've noticed that you're attracted to bad boys. If I turn off my virus software and stop backing up my hard drive, would you go out with me?"

The Power of Peer Pressure

It's almost impossible to overstate the influence of peer relationships on the behavior of most teenagers. The peer structure in your youth group has important effects on friendship patterns, social behavior, and achievement of the young people. The degree to which a young person is liked or disliked by others in the youth group will shape how she feels about herself. Her social position in relation to others has a direct bearing on her attitudes toward herself and toward others in the youth group. Furthermore, her perception of her relative position in the peer group structure often determines how the student will use her ability in the youth group. Someone who sees herself as well liked will tend to express more positive feelings toward self, others, and the youth group. The young person who sees herself as disliked tends to express more negative feelings.

Social life can make or break a teen's self-esteem. All the adulation and love in the world from one's parents and youth leaders may not mean as much as a feeling of acceptance from one's peers. Being a social outcast can seriously influence a teen's behavior in youth group. Teens who don't fit in may appear lazy, bored, or uninterested.

Jen was a member of our youth group who always appeared to be aloof and reserved. She attended almost every youth activity, but she seemed to cling near the adult leaders, preferring to help them rather than participating in activities with her peers. When one of our leaders heard a couple of other members of the group planning a weekend trip to the movies, the youth leader casually suggested they invite Jen and several other kids. That was the turning point for Jen. She began to emerge from her shell and felt far more comfortable with the youth group once she knew she was accepted. All it took was a little nudging on the part of a concerned adult leader.

You see, if you're a young person who feels insecure about your own worth, then you'll be extremely threatened by the possibility of ridicule or rejection by your peers. You'll be more sensitive about being laughed at. You'll lack the confidence to be different. Your problems seem bad enough without making them worse by defying the wishes of the majority. So you'll dress the way they tell you to dress, you'll talk the way they tell you to talk, and you'll think the way they want you to think (or at least you'll keep quiet if you think differently). All these behaviors have one thing in common: They result from feelings of inferiority.

Young people who can't fit in with one social group may find another group to hang out with, but they may never really feel comfortable there. These kids may seem to have perceptual chips on their shoulders and may bad-mouth the group they really wish would accept them. The inability to fit in can often lead to very negative outlooks toward both school and church.

Positive Peer Pressure

We are all aware of how youth group members encourage and reinforce a problem student's disruptive behavior. This negative peer pressure is often a major contribution to troublesome behavior. But peer pressure in a positive direction can be a great tool for getting young people to "clean up their acts" and improve their behavior.

You can help build an atmosphere of positive peer pressure by enlisting the aid of key group members. Choose kids with emotional and spiritual maturity, and encourage these student leaders to exert their influence for the good of group members and the ministry as a whole.

One example of how positive peer pressure worked in our group involved a student we'll call Bill. Bill wasn't a bad kid, but he was always getting into some kind of minor trouble. When we went to Tijuana to distribute food and clothing, Bill bought fireworks and tried to sneak them back across the border. In Sunday school, when it was time to break into small groups for discussion, he was always the last one to drag himself over to his group—or he'd explain how he could participate from outside the circle and didn't really need to move. We tried a wide variety of methods to get Bill involved, with little success, until we encouraged a few of our student leaders to simply say positive things about him when he did participate. He would get this little grin on his face—a somewhat surprised "I-did-good" look. With that encouragement, Bill started to share more often in the discussions, and even volunteered to lead the conversation one week.

Here are a few specific ways you can use positive peer pressure to guide your students:

• **Form peer-support groups.** Have kids meet in groups of no more than five to discuss their problems, brainstorm solutions, and pray for one another. The adult leader in these groups acts as a facilitator, encourager, and affirmer. This is not the time to give a speech or a lecture, though it is appropriate for adult leaders to remind students about the truth of how they are loved by both the leader and by God. Adult leaders need to live their life with appropriate transparency in front of the students, being honest about struggles while avoiding the kind of uncensored sharing of failures that amounts to emotional exhibitionism. Transparency can make students feel emotionally safe. C. S. Lewis wrote, "Friendship is born at that moment when one person says to another: 'What! You, too? I thought I was the only one.'" Peer-support groups provide an opportunity for you to get to know kids on an intimate level. The groups also provide a place for young people to "let their hair down."

• **Provide peer-counselor training.** Barbara Varenhorst at the National Peer Ministry Center has developed a peer-counseling model that trains young people in listening skills, questioning skills, ways to negotiate with adults, and ways to help one another. Barbara's program provides tools to help kids help one another with their problems and teaches kids better interpersonal skills for communicating with parents, teachers, and peers. For more information on Barbara's peer-counseling program and other efforts, visit www.peerministry.org.

• **Let students establish and enforce the rules.** Since many young people make a game out of breaking rules to challenge authority, it can be helpful to place responsibility for making and enforcing rules on the young people themselves. This approach uses peer pressure to maintain disciplinary order and has worked well in some settings, though it's not without its challenges. (We'll talk more about how to involve students in setting ministry rules in chapter 6.)

The Need for Attention

One of the main reasons students misbehave is the need to gain attention.

If a student receives more attention from acting in destructive ways than from being well behaved, why should he want to conform? Attention gained in any manner is better than no attention at all.

In *How to Discipline with Love*, Dr. Fitzhugh Dodson uses the law of the soggy potato chip to talk about a young person's need for attention. The law goes like this: If someone is given the choice between a fresh potato chip and a soggy one, he'll almost always choose the fresh one. But if the choice is between a soggy potato chip and no potato chip at all, he'll settle for the soggy one. Applying this concept to youth ministry, most young people would prefer an adult youth leader's positive attention to negative attention. But if the choice is between an adult's negative attention and no attention at all, teenagers will usually choose the negative attention. To most young people, any kind of attention—even negative attention—is better than being ignored.

Adult youth leaders tend to direct lots of attention toward misbehaving students in an effort to get these kids to toe the line. This negative attention may include threats, lectures, or displays of anger and frustration toward the young person. Adult leaders intend such negative attention as a form of discipline. But, strangely enough, to a misbehaving young person it may act as a reward. Their misbehavior turns the youth leader's attention toward them. The result is that many adult leaders are teaching their young people the exact opposite of what they want them to learn.

The primary difference between motivated and turned-off students is not the need for attention, but the way these students have learned to get attention.

Positive attention naturally falls to those who do well. On the other hand, negative attention naturally falls to those who have problems. Because students will seek to get attention one way or another, give them the kind that is helpful—praise and encouragement for doing the right things. (We'll talk more about this in chapter 5.)

Walk the Talk

No matter what we say about how we hope kids will behave, they will learn far more from what we do. The rule of effective modeling is simple: Walk the talk. In other words, as an adult youth leader it is essential to act as you would have your students act. If you want them to treat one another with respect and kindness, treat them with respect and kindness. If you want them to listen when you talk, listen when they talk. If your students experience you saying one thing but doing another, they are far more likely to believe—and learn from—what they see you doing.

Over the next several days, monitor your actions, your language, and your attitudes. Look for inconsistencies, places where you might be able to bring your behavior more in line with your expectations for your kids—even if it's for no other reason than to justify asking the same in return from them. No matter what kids hear you say, the real message they'll hear is conveyed by your actions.

Now Ask Yourself

1. Why should a young person behave in your youth group?

2. How do you respond genuinely to your people's moods and feelings without being manipulated or overwhelmed by them?

3. Describe some of the emotions/feelings you have seen in your young people this last week. How do you respond to these emotions?

4. Are there young people in your group who do not feel wanted? What can be done to help them?

5. What was your experience of peer pressure during your teenage years? Can you remember times when peers had a negative influence on your behavior? How about times when peers were a positive influence?

6. What does a young person have to do to get your attention?

© 1985 Rob Portlock

"OK, OK. We'll go to Disneyland."

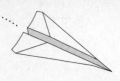

4

Giving Kids Confidence to Be All God Wants Them to Be

It's easy to forget that discipline is intended for our young people's benefit, not for our own. I have to be careful that I am not merely trying to create a showpiece. Do I care too much what others think about my kids and their reflection on me? Is the discipline I'm doing really something that will help my young people grow and mature, or is it just about getting kids to listen to what I say? All discipline and punishment should be done to help my young people be their best, not make me look good or give me fewer problems.

As adult youth leaders we must accept personal responsibility for some of what goes on in our youth group. Sometimes I can be my own worst enemy. When I lose my temper, raise my voice, or put a kid down, I lose my credibility, build up barriers, and tear down a kid's self-esteem. It helps to ask ourselves how much we are contributing to the discipline problems we experience.

There's a story about a ship that was trying to make its way on a dark, foggy night. All of a sudden the captain saw a bright light directly in his ship's path. The captain flashed a message to the approaching ship: "Change your course 10 degrees to the north."

Within a few seconds a message came back to the captain, "Change your course 10 degrees to the south."

Well, that irritated the captain, so he sent out another message to this approaching ship: "I am a captain. Change your course 10 degrees to the north."

He got another message back: "I'm a Seaman 3rd Class. Change your course 10 degrees to the south."

This infuriated the captain, so he sent out a third message as he maintained his path directly toward the oncoming light: "I'm a battleship. Change your course 10 degrees to the north."

He got another message back. "I'm a lighthouse. Change your course 10 degrees to the south."

Sometimes we are the ones who need to shift direction if we want to make a difference in the lives of kids. I used to pray, "Lord, change my kids," and nothing seemed to happen. But when I began to pray, "Lord, change me," I started to see my kids in a different light.

Great Expectations

To start building your positive disciplinarian skills, try this little exercise. Think about the various activities involved in a typical gathering of your youth group. As you consider each part of the meeting, imagine how your youth group would look if every student were mature and cooperative. (Am I asking the impossible?) Picture what the group is like when every single youth is motivated and responsible. Once you envision how you would like young people to participate in activities, you are on your way to teaching young people to meet your positive expectations.

Gordon MacDonald explains that there are two ways to paddle a canoe through white water. You can wait until you get into the rapids to decide what you're going to do, but you'll probably end up falling into the water. The other way is to keep your eyes 50 yards downstream, picking your route in advance so you know exactly how you're going to act before you get there. Many adult youth leaders make the mistake of never planning ahead not thinking about what kind of young people they hope to produce.

When I was younger, I was taught that if you have high expectations of young people, you'll always be disappointed. But that's not necessarily true; in fact, it often works just the opposite way. When people know you have high expectations of them, they have more incentive to perform well. This fact is supported by a study cited by Warren Bennis in *The Unconscious Conspiracy: Why Leaders Can't Lead*. Bennis refers to a study of schoolteachers that concluded that when teachers held high expectations of their students, that alone was enough to cause an increase of 25 points in the students' IQ scores.

It was Ralph Waldo Emerson who said, "Our chief want in life is someone who will make us do what we can." Our job as adult youth leaders is to give kids confidence God is working in and through them. Always remember you are dealing with ordinary kids in the hands of the extraordinary God. We need to communicate to young people that we have confidence in them.

Unfortunately, our words sometimes communicate the exact opposite. Learn to avoid these and other negative words and phrases which tend to discourage young people:

"Let me finish that for you."
"You are too slow."
"I'm ashamed of you."
"There isn't any excuse for this."
"Can't you do anything right?"
"Did you mess that up again?"
"When will you ever learn?"
"What's the matter with you?"

It's odd how constant faultfinding can make a young person deaf. He learns to turn off the criticism because he knows what type of comments he is going to hear. If you are given to blaming, ridiculing, teasing, or sarcasm, then stop it. No one likes this kind of behavior. Faultfinding is self-defeating; when you have a legitimate criticism, the young person is unlikely to heed it. He has heard too many picky statements he knows were not valid. Faultfinding does not usually change a person's behavior on a long-term basis. It may sometimes produce immediate results, but lasting results are rare.

Remember that every one of your kids is a mixture of good qualities and bad ones. If you tend to label your young people—each student is either motivated or lazy, smart or dumb, charming or challenging—

you minimize who they all are as individuals. Try to see all the kids you work with as real people with both positive and negative qualities. Then you can help them overcome the negative while building on the positive qualities. We need to treat our kids in ways that reflect our highest expectations of all they are and all they can become.

Some adult youth leaders never expect their young people to amount to much, and those leaders are seldom disappointed. But when you believe in your kids, they'll rise to your expectations. Don't stifle their desire to succeed by telling them they can't. Instead, let your positive attitude rub off on them.

Ten Qualities of a Positive Disciplinarian

Below you'll find descriptions of some basic inner qualities that are important for those who have authority over young people. As you study these characteristics of a positive disciplinarian, try to identify the areas needing improvement in your own life.

1. Integrity. Adult youth leaders must set the example of how they want their group to behave. You are the blueprint for the kids you work with. "Students are not above their teacher, but all who are fully trained will be like their teacher" (Luke 6:40). Young people desperately need mature adult models who live out their beliefs. What we do speaks much louder than what we say.

John Wooden, former UCLA basketball coach, is certainly an example of this. Every player who served under him has made the same comment. Whatever Coach Wooden asked them to do, he always did himself. If the players had to be in the motel at a certain time, Wooden was in the motel at that same time. There were no double standards with him. He practiced what he preached.

2. Honesty. Youth ministry demands that we be honest with our kids and with ourselves. And that includes being willing to admit our own mistakes.

When you make a mistake, don't try to cover it up and make excuses. If you expect honesty from your kids, set the example yourself. Don't be afraid to say, "I was wrong, I'm sorry." This isn't always easy. Sometimes we are afraid of showing weakness and inadequacy that may make us appear less than leaders.

I found myself struggling with the need to admit my own mistake late one Sunday evening as our youth group was returning from a trip to the beach. We'd had a great experience—complete with campfire, wonderful singing, and a powerful prayer time. On the way home the bus suddenly stopped and wouldn't start. (We found out later it was simply out of gas). The kids were just being themselves—talking and laughing; they didn't care that we were going to be late getting home. But all I could think of were the 60 sets of parents waiting for us.

As the bus driver tried to figure out our problem, he couldn't hear the engine turn over due to the noise on the bus. He asked the kids to be quiet, and the few who heard his feeble appeal did quiet down. But the others hadn't heard his request, so they kept talking and giggling.

At this point I lost my cool. I was tired, eager to get home, and embarrassed that we were going to be late. I started yelling about how rude they were with all their noise. (You must understand I'm not normally a yeller.) It got deadly quiet on the bus as I ranted and raved for about five minutes. The minute I stepped out of the bus I realized how I had overreacted to a minor situation. I got back on the bus, which was still deadly quiet—the kids were in shock from my outburst—and I apologized to them. As difficult as it was to admit I was wrong, the incident drew us closer—and not because the kids now knew that even the youth minister could blow it occasionally. (I'm positive they already knew this!) It brought us closer because I wasn't afraid to admit my failure and ask for their forgiveness.

3. Wisdom. Pray for wisdom as a disciplinarian. A lot is left up to your judgment. Sometimes you'll be forced to make decisions quickly in a difficult situation where you'll have lots of questions to consider:

- What happened?
- Who is responsible?
- What were the circumstances?
- What was the motive?
- Is the responsible person repentant?
- What kind of discipline is necessary?

My need for wisdom was glaringly apparent one evening when I walked into the youth building and heard the sound of breaking glass. I ran to the bathroom where the noise had come from, and discovered pieces of broken mirror scattered all over the floor. I also found a guilty-looking high school guy with skin torn from his knuckles. Sherlock Holmes fan that I am, I used some elementary deduction and concluded the young man had broken the mirror with his fist. (And you thought youth ministers were only good at volleyball.)

This particular young man had a bad track record and was consistently getting in trouble. I was ready to pounce on him for this senseless act of vandalism. Instead I sent up a quick prayer and began asking non-threatening questions to find out what had happened. It turned out this guy's girlfriend was going out with someone else. Instead of hitting the new boyfriend, he'd hit the mirror—not intending to break it.

I said very little. He knew what he'd done was wrong, and he was sorry. We cleaned up the broken mirror together, and he did extra jobs around the church the next month to pay for a new mirror. We became friends during that time, and I was able to use that opportunity to share with him about the Lord. I'm still grateful for God's wisdom in handling a potentially volatile situation.

4. Patience. All youth leaders need a large measure of patience. Remember, these are kids. If they were perfect, then you wouldn't be needed. You would be out of a job. I love the slogan that's sometime seen on T-shirts: "Be patient: God isn't finished with me yet!" Our kids are growing and changing, and we need to be patient, knowing that God continues to work in their lives.

Teenagers are not little adults. Many times they handle situations poorly. That's one of the reasons you are around—to guide and teach them ways to handle anger, frustration, bitterness, and exasperation. I'm not saying we have to be perfect in the area of patience, but let's hope we're a little further along on this than the kids we're teaching.

Just as love can cover a multitude of sins, impatience can destroy months of ministry. A single untimely outburst or overreaction can cause some young people to cross an adult youth leader off their lists for months. We have to work hard to avoid the kinds of hot-tempered outbursts that can set back our relationships with our students.

5. Teamwork. The entire youth ministry staff must believe in and reinforce the same rules; staff members must stand behind one another. If they don't, young people will soon find the "weakest link"—the adult who's easiest to sway. If adult youth leaders disagree about how to handle a particular situation, they need to get behind closed doors and say, "Even though we don't agree on the best response here, let's agree that it's more important for the young people's welfare that we be united than it is for anyone's opinion to prevail."

One year we took an extremely rowdy and hyperactive group of high school guys on a camping trip. They were in a tent with an inexperienced counselor. (That was our first mistake.) Before the trip began, our leadership team had agreed that when it was time for lights out, we would keep all our campers in their tents for the rest of the night. This particular counselor, however, decided the best way to get the kids in his tent to like him was to let them run around "for only 10 minutes" after lights out. After running around for a little while, they got a little more daring and started pulling up tent pegs of other campers and throwing food around the camp. This went on for 25 minutes. The guys not only scared the rest of our group, but also disturbed many other people who were camping at this public campground. The park ranger eventually quieted things down, but our reputation was shattered, and we'd lost any chance to have a positive impact for the Lord at that campground.

Young people need to see unity among their adult leaders. There cannot be one leader openly dissenting. It's like a football team; it's better for everyone to execute the play the quarterback calls than for half the team to do one thing and half to do another.

Be loyal to those in positions of authority over you. If the senior minister or church board makes a rule you don't like, talk to them privately. Don't debate the rightness or wrongness of the rules in front of your young people. Don't paint the senior pastor or church board as the bad guys by saying things like, "They gave us this dumb rule. I hate it too, but we have to do it." You do neither the young people nor those in authority any good by such off-the-record remarks. Discipline has to be a team effort.

6. Consistency. Consistency is the backbone of discipline. Inconsistent or contradictory discipline is more confusing and harmful to a young person than the extremes of too much or too little discipline. No form of discipline is useful unless the leaders are definite, firm, and consistent in what they ask and forbid.

Sometimes a warning acts as a challenge to young people. They'll do what you've warned against just to see if you'll carry out your threat. They know what the penalty is, and they're ready to risk it, just to test you.

I remember one summer when some students of mine took the challenge of breaking camp rules on the last night before we were headed home. The last night of summer camp is always the most difficult as far as keeping kids in their cabins after lights out. The campers know they'll be going home the next morning, so they figure there's not a lot the camp leaders can do to discipline them if they are caught.

The guys in my cabin that year were a lot of fun, though they were always getting into something. Maybe that's what made them so much fun. They were into everything and they were lively. Unfortunately for these guys, I overheard their plan to get up in the middle of the night and raid the girls' cabins. That night, when they thought I was asleep, they began to wake one another up, hardly making a sound. They were good at it! I could barely hear them whispering as they dressed silently in the darkness of the cabin. It took them about 10 minutes to put on their warm clothes and tiptoe over to the cabin's only door.

When I heard the hand on the doorknob, I quietly but firmly cut through the darkness of the room with, "Everybody back in bed, now!" For the next two minutes (which seemed like forever) there was no movement, and I could tell it was a standoff. I could hear a couple of them whispering, calculating the odds. Obviously, there was little chance I could physically stop the 12 of them from leaving the room. I could hear them questioning what I could and would do. I repeated my message one more time, and it was followed by another long silence. Then, one by one, they went back to their beds. I knew they were disappointed their plan was foiled, so I told them what a great plan it was and how they'd almost gotten me. We started talking about it and had a great laugh. They knew I was on their side, but they also knew I'd be consistent about enforcing the rules, even on the last night of camp.

Mean what you say. Don't beg kids to behave. You cannot be wishy-washy if you want to be effective. Kids can spot hesitancy a mile away. If you are uncertain, they will work on you and wear you down.

You should never threaten consequences you are not willing to carry out. When you've issued a warning, be sure to see it through. Young people need to know you'll respond consistently and unemotionally to misbehavior. You can expect that young people will test you to find out if you mean what you say. As young people realize you are going to be consistent in implementing the consequences you've established, they will abandon this type of testing behavior.

Consistency means no exceptions—not even for the senior pastor's son or the daughter of your church board chairperson. It means enforcing the rules even when there are only five minutes left in class. If you aren't consistent with only five minutes left, next week they'll start acting up with ten minutes left. Values and moral standards simply cannot be taught without consistent discipline.

Every Youth Worker's Nightmare Come True

7. Flexibility. While it's very important to be consistent, this must be balanced with a flexibility that takes into account that every kid is different. You need to choose your battles wisely, or you'll find you're battling all the time. You could be ticked off at teens 24 hours a day. There's always some kid doing something that will drive you up the wall. As William James said, "The art of being wise is to know what to overlook." Save your energy for the things that matter. Ask yourself, "Is this worth going to the mat over?" If you get mad and scream and yell and make a big deal out of every little problem, you won't be heard when you really need to be heard. Don't risk fracturing your relationships with kids over behavior that has no moral significance. There are plenty of real issues that will require you to stand like a rock. Try to be sensitive to individual needs and don't make a major deal out of minor infractions.

In the book *Growing Pains in the Classroom*, Frank Johns shares a memory from his own adolescence that illustrates the importance of a leader's flexibility in responding to different individual situations:

My algebra teacher was Brother Albertus—known for his quick temper and the occasional use of physical force on students. I either did not have time to study one day, or I was just trying to see if I could get away with something, so I copied the formula for the binominal expansion on a cheat sheet and planned to use it on the test.

I remember the excitement as I sat in class and slipped out the cheat sheet, while Brother Albertus walked along the rows of desks. The combination of fear and excitement is still very close to me as I write this story. Then somehow he saw me cheating. I don't remember how it happened, or how I could have been so careless, but he caught me. Brother Albertus came up to the desk and I was really scared—scared of physical punishment, scared of embarrassment, and scared my parents would find out. I was rooted to the desk, wondering what my fate would be, looking at him, unable to say a word. He moved my test paper, and then marked no credit with his pen for the one problem.

Brother Albertus never mentioned the incident to me afterwards, never told anyone else, and gave no indications to the class it had happened. Many times as a teacher, when I was in a position similar to that of Brother Albertus, I remembered this incident. I had "learned a lesson" in honesty without being humiliated or punished. The fact that the teacher knew and I knew what happened was punishment enough. Finally, I learned that if rules or laws, either in school or elsewhere in society, are broken, I have to deal with each case individually and not just "go by the book."

"When my parents are busy criticizing my hair, they forget to criticize my grades, music, friends, and personality."

8. Accountability. Just as it's important for us as leaders to be accountable for our own actions, we also need to encourage that same quality in our kids. Sometimes this can mean allowing our kids to fail so they can learn from their mistakes.

I'm quite sure the father in Jesus' parable of the prodigal son (Luke 15) tried to reason with his son before the son took off with his share of the estate. But once the son left, his father allowed him to be responsible for his own welfare, even when things didn't turn out too well. The father desperately hoped his son would return, but he didn't send people to drag him back or additional money to make sure he was free from need. The father let his son experience hunger, filth, and failure before he eventually came home. The youth leader who is too anxious to bail young people out of difficulty may be doing them a disservice by depriving them of the experience of failure.

Ezekiel 18:20 clearly says each of us is accountable for his or her own actions: "The one who sins is the one who will die. The child will not share the guilt of the parent, nor will the parent share the guilt of the child. The righteousness of the righteous will be credited to them, and the wickedness of the wicked will be charged against them." Your young people will experience pain and suffering as a result of their sins;

Scripture teaches we are morally accountable as individuals. Let students learn from their mistakes, take responsibility for them, and mature in the process.

Challenge your kids to take risks, even if it sometimes means failure. There are constructive lessons to be learned from failure, and failure can spur people on to impressive accomplishments if they continue trying and don't give up and stop trying. The Wright Brothers failed in many attempts to make a flying machine; Winston Churchill was widely regarded as a political failure in his early career; Willie Mays got only one hit in his first 26 major league at bats. As long as failure doesn't become a way of life, it is nothing to be ashamed of.

9. A Sense of Humor. Don't take youth ministry too seriously. I know full well how exhausting youth ministry is, how it tests your mettle to the nth degree, and how important it is to be a good adult leader. But that doesn't mean you should never crack a smile. Young people can be hilarious—and so can our own struggles to deal with them effectively! Never be afraid to laugh at yourself. Laugh with your young people. Laughter can drown a multitude of sorrows and tension. The world has enough gloomy, frowning faces; bring a smile to your youth group and share it with your kids.

Sometimes you have to laugh with kids just so you don't kill them! Bob Merrill, minister of youth at a Presbyterian church in New Jersey, tells the story of a heart-stopping experience he had during an overnight retreat at a mountain cabin. In the evening the guys and girls departed to their respective rooms. Bob woke up early one morning and realized he was alone in his room. When he went to the living room, he found the entire youth group sleeping in the living room of the cabin with no supervision. As he counted heads (or toes, depending on what was showing from under the sleeping bags), his eyes came to the middle of the floor. His heart grew faint as he saw four feet protruding from the end of an unzipped and folded-over sleeping bag. He could see the headlines: "Youth Minister Arrested after Retreat Orgy." As he was about to let them have it with both barrels, he rolled back the sleeping bag and found Tom and Sam staring back at him. "Good morning, Bob," they yelled. "Got ya!" They'd gotten him, and he knew it! He and the entire youth group had a great laugh.

Having a sense of humor doesn't just mean you can take a joke. It also means you can say, "All right, I made a mistake, but it didn't wipe me out." Young people need to know that failure isn't fatal, and that being Christian doesn't mean we're always perfect.

Youth leaders with a good sense of humor aren't afraid to let their barriers down. They are able to relax and enjoy being with young people, and this helps youth be truly comfortable around them. Being able to see humor even in difficult situations can ease tension and stress and help get us through trying times. For adults who work with youth, a good sense of humor is not just an option—it's a prerequisite. Proverbs 17:22 says, "A cheerful heart is good medicine." Adult leaders need to be able to apply that medicine to the troubled spirits of today's young people.

If you are unwilling or unable to smile or find humor in the daily turmoil of life with students, then you are definitely in the wrong line of work! Nonetheless, it's important to be careful how you use humor. If you tease, give kids a hard time, or criticize kids and disguise it as joking, don't be angry when your young people do the same. You may be tempted to come up with a clever line to embarrass a kid who's misbehaving, but these words can be cruel and demeaning. They send the message to a young person that "If you want to play cutthroat, I'm older and sharper than you are." Don't put a young person down and create a negative atmosphere. Don't nail him with derogatory remarks. Don't tear her down as a person.

10. The Most Important Quality: Love. Even in the ideal atmosphere, with the best programs, there can still be problem youth. When the rowdies surface, the first thing to do is try to develop a relationship with them. We can't effectively discipline someone we don't know. We have to earn the right to be heard, and we do that by spending time with those kids—visiting them in their homes, meeting them for pizza after school, or attending their band concerts or basketball games.

How do you help rowdy kids? The same way you help anyone else—love them! Love them until you begin to understand them. Then love them some more—until they know you've begun to understand them.

I have always been convinced just about any form of discipline can be effective as long as it is firmly grounded in a genuine love for your young people. A loving adult youth leader disciplines with a heart filled with compassion.

Unconditional love will help young people see themselves as significant and important to God. Look at every kid in your youth group as having potential—even the kid who drives you up the wall. You know the kid I mean—the one you secretly pray will not show up at your next meeting, yet he's there sitting in the front row every week. That kid who needs your love. Remember, the kids who are sharp enough to get into trouble are probably creative enough to become significant. Don't focus only on who a young person is right now, but on who he or she can become.

Never deprive a young person in a way that will make her feel unloved. Never say, "I don't love you when…" or "I won't love you if…" Never use the "silent treatment"—which only deprives the young person of your love and care for the time you don't talk to him.

Perhaps you should spend some more time establishing with your young people relationships grounded in respect and love, and less time worrying about blind obedience. Love is still the greatest motive for obedience. Love your young people unconditionally. Love your young people because you should love them, not as a way to get what you want. If your love is compelling, your young people will love you back. And unless there are competitive forces pulling harder than your love, you'll find your kids will be much more likely to obey you—not because they must, but because they desire to.

In every youth group there must be affection, and a lot of it. I am talking about real, down-to-earth, sincere love. The kind that carries conviction through a caring pat on the shoulder, through the gentle tone of the voice, through the fond look that says as clearly as words, "I love you for what you are, beyond anything you might do. I love you because you are you." This kind of atmosphere can weather the storms of conflict that come up in every youth group.

Loving your kids includes being aware of what's going on in their lives. Maybe the girl who is acting up has parents who fight constantly and are considering a divorce. She may be living with a mother who is exhausted and trying to hold things together. She may sense rejection from her father. She may hear her parents yelling and screaming at each other over the phone each evening. Unfortunately, she will not be wearing a sign as she enters your youth group that says, "Go easy on me today."

You must let your young people know they are valuable to you. Your kids need to know you love them, so when a reprimand is needed, it is not mistaken as a loss of love. You must also communicate that you are reprimanding a person's behavior, not his or her character. What a difference there is between saying, "You lied," and "You are a liar."

Closely linked with being loved should come the knowledge of belonging to some bigger whole. Seek to create a sense of togetherness within your youth group, a sense of being united with others, not isolated or alone. Create an atmosphere that gives young people the security of knowing they belong.

Each and every one of us, young people and youth leaders alike, have a deep desire to feel accepted and understood. We need desperately to be able to share our thoughts and feelings with one person, or several people, who really understand. We yearn for the deep relief of knowing we can be ourselves, secure in the knowledge that says, "This person is with me. He accepts how I feel!"

Communicating Love to Young People

To be effective as positive disciplinarians, we must love all our young people just the way they are. In order to love them we must get beyond surface relationships. We need to be their friends. When our young people sense we have made an effort to really get to know them as individuals, they will listen more intently to what we have to say.

But how do we let kids know we love them? My good friend Dick

Gibson wrote an article for *Group* magazine several years ago in which he described 55 ways to love your kids:

1. **Remember names.** Few things leave a more lasting impression on kids than your ability to call them by name!

2. **Meet at the kids' level.** Position yourself to communicate at eye level. Also take care that your vocabulary is easily understood by your teenagers.

3. **Send birthday cards.** Who sends young people cards? Immediate family, extended relatives, and close friends. Why not add your name to that list?

4. **Invite them along.** Never go anywhere alone. Asking one or more kids to join you confirms their worth to you. And it's a great chance to share informally and to model the Christian life.

5. **Be in touch.** How many kids suffered through another week without any positive physical contact? Expressions as simple as a hand on the shoulder or a "holy hug" can prove your concern.

6. **Respond to absences.** Many young people drop out if they feel unneeded or unimportant. When you follow up with them, it communicates their value to you and the group.

7. **Forgive and forget.** First Corinthians 13:5 says love "keeps no record of wrongs." If you model authentic forgiveness, it'll give your kids the courage to do the same.

8. **Recognize accomplishments.** Look for opportunities to applaud your group members. Spread the word to family and friends you want to know about this inside information.

9. **Write encouraging notes.** Kids love to get mail, so send them brief postcards or letters. Express your confidence in them and reaffirm your availability.

10. **Offer support in a crisis.** You're never more needed than when your teenagers face trouble. When kids face unexpected pregnancy, abuse, crime, death, or rejection, your active concern can impact them for a lifetime.

11. **Recognize personality changes.** Abrupt shifts from normal behavior patterns may be signals that a kid needs help. Don't

hesitate to share your concern.

12. **Follow up on prayer requests.** Ask for progress reports on prayer concerns. This reminds your kids that you take their spiritual lives seriously and helps them recognize God's provision.

13. **Use the telephone.** How often do you phone your teenagers for no reason? Call just to say "Hi!"

14. **Go to their "natural habitat."** Your presence on your group members' turf is significant. So go to school events or visit the places they work.

15. **Open your home.** Occasionally, ask kids to join you at home apart from regular group activities.

16. **Confront in love.** Authentic concern sometimes says, "I care for you too much to let that continue." Your willingness to deal with tough issues reveals the true nature of your commitment. (See Hebrews 12:5-11.)

17. **Listen.** You don't need all the answers, just two good ears. Empower your teenagers to talk through their problems with someone they can trust.

18. **Answer questions.** Young people have difficulty interpreting the mixed messages they receive. If they ask, it's because they trust you. Don't be afraid to respond honestly, even in sensitive areas.

19. **Say "I love you!"** These words can never be said too often. Say them personally, sincerely, and individually.

20. **Affirm spiritual growth.** Everyone can use a spiritual "pat on the back." Commend godly character you observe.

21. **"Unwrap" kids' giftedness.** When you detect latent talents or abilities in your kids, give them encouragement and opportunities to explore those gifts.

22. **Expect the best.** Young people will settle to your level of expectation—so aim high.

23. **Accept them as they are.** Teenagers are in transition from childhood to adulthood, and they can act like either at any moment. Be patient—God's not finished with them (or you, for that matter).

24. **Focus on their interests.** Investigate your group members'

hobbies and ask for pointers. They'll be happy to oblige, and you'll gain new insights into them.

25. **Be available.** Inform your group that you're accessible when they need you. (Remember to tell them when you're not available, too.) You lose opportunities to minister if you allow kids to weather their storms alone.

26. **Laugh together.** Don't be so serious that you miss humorous moments.

27. **Cultivate kids' opinions.** Invite honest feedback and keep an open mind. God may want your young people to teach you something.

28. **Be real.** Your teenagers hunger for relationships with people who have the confidence to be themselves.

29. **Be a "soft touch."** When you can, participate in your kids' fundraisers. To avoid going broke, I purchase only from the first group member who asks me to.

30. **Speak first.** Initiating conversation can be difficult for shy or new group members. Make them feel important by speaking to them first.

31. **Give positive reinforcement.** Some young people are lightning rods for criticism. So look for something praiseworthy in every group member.

32. **Keep confidences.** Develop a reputation as someone who's reliable with confidential information. Nothing is more destructive to your credibility than breaking a trust.

33. **Share "good news."** When group members make the news, mail them the clippings. Even if their parents already have a supply for the relatives, they'll appreciate your thoughtfulness.

34. **Seek sanctuary.** Your meetings should not be a battleground for personal disputes. Place a high priority on emotional security and acceptance for everyone.

35. **Be dependable.** How's your track record for consistency? If you're reliable in the small things you'll be rewarded with greater confidence.

36. **Be a servant.** Greatness, as Jesus demonstrated, is expressed through service. Your group will reflect this truth to the extent they observe it in you.

37. **Send postcards.** When you travel, mail postcards about your experience to your group members. Let them know that even though you're away, they're still on your mind.

38. **Smile.** Your smile expresses openness and approachability.

39. **Watch your tone of voice.** Clear communication includes both the words we choose and how we express them. Take care that your tone reflects concern and support.

40. **Be attentive.** It's frustrating to talk with someone whose actions demonstrate they're not interested. Make sure your body language reflects concern.

41. **Support through prayer.** Select two or three group members to pray for every week. Inform them in advance and ask for special needs or requests.

42. **Maintain eye contact.** The eyes are a window to the soul. So let your kids see your compassion in your eyes.

43. **Watch your words.** Real affection is often exercised through what we decide not to say. Your careless remarks could leave lasting scars.

44. **Post kids' pictures.** Ask each group member for a school photo. Exhibit these photos in a high-profile place.

45. **Give kids respect.** This is a "boomerang principle"—give and you will receive in return.

46. **Take them seriously.** Don't brush off your kids' problems or concerns, no matter how trivial they might seem.

47. **Admit your mistakes.** Don't be fooled. We're usually the last to acknowledge what others already know.

48. **Avoid church/school conflicts.** Arbitrary scheduling that forces kids to choose between church and school activities is unfair.

49. **Foster teamwork.** Although your role will always involve overseeing the tasks at hand, don't lose touch with the crew. Serving together in the trenches builds camaraderie.

50. **Invest your time in them.** There's no substitute for just being together. This life-to-life interaction is the essence of discipleship.

51. **Smooth "rough" edges.** Do you have kids who lack social graces or need help with personal hygiene? It's awkward, but that's what friends are for.

52. **Visit them at home.** A young person's room is his or her corner of the world and your turnstile to it. Make an appointment and ask for a "guided tour."

53. **Empathize.** Empathy is "feeling your pain in my heart." Isn't this how Jesus expressed his love for us? Remember what it is like to be a kid.

54. **Play together.** If your teenagers would rather watch than participate, help them rediscover the joy of play. Choose activities that stress total group participation.

55. **Resist favoritism.** If pressed, you'd admit feeling "closer" to some kids than others. Budget your time and attention to everyone equally.

Now Ask Yourself

1. What is your motivation for wanting well-disciplined young people?

2. Besides "boring," describe what your youth group would be like if you only had mature and cooperative young people?

3. What are your expectations of your young people?

4. Who in your life encouraged you to pursue your dreams as a teen? How did they do it?

5. What negative phrases do you need to cut back on or eliminate in talking with young people.

6. Each of us wears different hats in youth ministry. The list below includes some of the roles youth workers often play. Overall, how do the young people in your youth group see you? Are you content with this opinion? If not, how can you change it?

   A. Police officer
   B. Firefighter
   C. Clown
   D. Scholar

   E. Just one of the kids
   F. Mother or father
   G. Babysitter

7. Is there a weak link on your team? How can this tactfully be corrected?

8. Are you able to laugh at yourself? Are you fun to be with? If not, what can you do to change?

9. Is your youth group a loving group? Do your kids feel wanted?

"Whadda you mean you need a vacation?
We thought hanging around us was your vacation."

5

Praise: Catch Them Doing Something Right

Working with loud, restless, adventurous youth is difficult—but I definitely prefer it to the alternative of working with silent, passive, unadventurous kids. I would rather try to calm a fanatic than raise a corpse any day!

It's been my experience that the kids who are creative enough to get into trouble are probably sharp enough to do something really significant with their lives. These kids are often the ones most in need of discipline seasoned with praise.

Amy Carmichael was one of those kids. When she was only 17, she began working with the poor children of Belfast. Later, while working in India, she saved the lives of countless children who were in danger of being sold as temple prostitutes and sacrifices. But listen to what biographer Elizabeth Elliott writes about Amy as a child:

> The eldest of seven children, she often led the rest of them in wild escapades, such as the time she suggested they all eat laburnum pods. She had been told the pods were poisonous, and thought it would be fun to see how long it would take them to die.

Or, take Brad—a kid from my youth group who was always giving us fits. He was the one who would take the clapper out of the camp bell, freeze the camp director's underwear in the freezer, or put goldfish in the camp pool. Brad got into all kinds of trouble, but I liked him. He was fun to be around, and I saw potential in him that others often could not.

One October we did a haunted house, and I put Brad in charge of the "operating room." It was terrific! Brad put in extra hours after school securing large bones, medical equipment, and doctors' outfits. He was wonderful at organizing his crew. Everyone pointed out what a great job he'd done. That haunted house—and the positive feedback he got about it—completely changed Brad's attitude about himself. He soon began using his abilities for the Lord in other areas, such as teaching the fourth-grade class. Brad is now a successful entrepreneur running his own business. He's still a character, but he's using his energy and creativity for the good of others.

A good way to motivate young people who have had behavior problems is to give them recognition when they start doing well. It is important to let young people know they are on target. Students need to know that you appreciate their efforts. Simple matter-of-fact positive feedback will not embarrass most high school students. It tells them you recognize their mature and responsible attitudes and actions.

The need for recognition is basic to every human being. It's one of the driving forces that keep us going and trying to do better. We especially want praise from people who are important to us.

Positive Feedback

Telling young people what they've done right is more important than telling them what they've done wrong. Tell young people how you see them growing and maturing and you'll see their faces light up. Speaking with kids about the positive qualities you see in them is one of the best ways to help them build positive self-images.

Our society tends to praise the four As:
- Appearance
- Academics
- Athletics
- Arts

I have no problem praising kids for their efforts in these four areas. But I feel it is far more important to give kids positive feedback for character traits that will last a lifetime. Positive character traits might include the following:

Cheerfulness	Honesty
Compassion	Humor
Courageousness	Kindness
Courtesy	Loyalty
Creativity	Organization
Decisiveness	Patience
Efficiency	Punctuality
Enthusiasm	Respect
Fair-mindedness	Self-discipline
Flexibility	Sincerity
Forgiving spirit	Sympathy
Friendliness	Thoughtfulness
Generosity	Understanding

Some adult youth leaders have the wrong motivation for praising young people. Praise isn't a tool to make you look good or to manipulate a kid's behavior. This is a big mistake. Students can spot phony praise a mile away. The goal of praise is to affirm and encourage students to grow and mature into the people God has created them to be.

Praising Improved Behavior

There is no more meaningful motivator than praise. When former UCLA Coach John Wooden was asked how he motivated his basketball players, he said, "I try to catch them doing something right." This isn't always easy in youth ministry! We can get so caught up in our frustrations and expectations surrounding our young people that we forget to praise them when we catch them doing something right.

Positive reinforcement is the key to effective discipline. Remember that all human beings need positive input. It takes only a few seconds to offer a kid in your youth group a word of praise or an affirming pat on the shoulder. But negative interactions are often time-consuming, exhausting, and disruptive. It is much more productive to commend a young person for doing something right than it is to wait for misbehavior to get your attention.

The young people in your group shouldn't have to do something extraordinary to win your praise. If you praise effort and progress now, the big things will come later. Praise is particularly valuable for a young person who is doing his level best at something that is especially hard for him.

These days, most of the reminders young people receive are focused on their problems. Kids hear about their mistakes from everyone. Think how much better off your young people will be if you give them positive reminders that, regardless of their failures, they are moving in the right direction.

It's been said that it takes six to eight compliments to make up for one criticism in a person's life. Sometimes our young people need a good locker room pep talk. Other times they need cheerleaders who stand on the sidelines—supporting, affirming, and encouraging them.

Look for intelligent, thoughtful questions asked by a student during a discussion. Keep your eyes peeled for a student putting someone else first—even if it's just something small like offering the last doughnut to somebody else. Listen for stories about good deeds kids have done away from the church setting, when no authority figures were watching.

By looking to praise your young people for good things, you are also training yourself to concentrate on the positive. Unfortunately, many youth leaders do the reverse. They are constantly on the lookout for things their young people are doing wrong, and ready to pounce on them. If misbehavior is the only thing you are looking for among your students, that's probably the only thing you'll find.

Emphasize Progress

I do much better with my young people when I remind myself that responsible behavior is not something that comes naturally. Responsibility is a social skill. Learning responsibility is desirable and leads to a better quality of life for everyone.

It's important to recognize progress and not simply the finished product. Young people become excited when they know you see them progressing in some good directions. Young people are more aware of their failures than we realize, and they are much less sure of their successes. When you see them making progress, tell them (and remind yourself) God is at work in their lives, and that you like what you see happening.

When I was in college, I was in a class taught by a visiting professor from another local school. Each day he would ask for comments on the assigned Bible passages, and I would often raise my hand and give my insights from the previous night's studying. I had studied hard and wanted to make a good impression on this professor. But his responses often caught me by surprise. Many times he not only would disagree with my answer but would belittle me in front of the class. He would comment on how no one with intelligence could possibly come up with an answer like mine. He also had a way of calling students he didn't like by their last names and students he liked by their first names. He would turn to me and say, "Now let's hear what Mr. Christie has to say on this subject." Maybe he thought this would get me to study even harder, but I became so discouraged that I stopped going to class. The thought of being made fun of in front of my peers was too great a threat. I have always prayed that I would remember that experience as an example of how not to teach my own students.

Paul Hauck, in *How to Do What You Want to Do: The Art of Self-Discipline*, emphasizes effort instead of achievement as a measure of success:

> It is more important to do than to do well. The main difficulties people have who are driven by perfection are that they have a faulty definition of success. To them success is doing something 100 percent okay and hardly anything less. It simply does not make sense to define success as near perfection. Think of success rather as a slight bit of improvement over what you were able to do before. Even if you are trying something and do not see improvement, you are still entitled

to say that you are improving, because the benefits of practice will show up later. As long as you are attempting something, improvement is being made. Even if your performance goes down, as it sometimes will, you can still learn from the experience. And that is the name of the game.

Parents occasionally slip into a performance-focused mode when responding to their teens. Maybe a student has a difficult time with math. So he starts putting in the effort to improve, spending less time with friends and hitting the books instead. On the next math test he brings home a B+. His parents lavishly praise him, letting him know how proud they are of him and his accomplishment. Then, after a long pause, one of them adds, "You know, with just a little more effort, I bet you could bring that up to an A." That last statement may be the only thing the student will remember. That final phrase wiped out all the positive words that came before it.

Ways to Praise

To get the most from your attempts to praise young people, try to offer positive feedback as soon as possible—shortly after the desired behavior has been accomplished. The payoff should be as immediate as possible. The faster the payoff, the more powerful it will be in strengthening the good behavior.

It's very important that your praise be specific. Use brief descriptive statements that tell young people the particular things you are affirming; don't just offer vague feedback telling them they did a nice job. Nonspecific praise creates praise "junkies" who are never really satisfied. In order for young people to repeat their good behavior, they need to know specifically what they have done right!

One common mistake people make in providing positive feedback is to overuse a pet phrase. To see if you do this, you may want to tape yourself as you lead a Bible study or when you are around the youth group. If you notice the same phrase four or five times, it is being overused. If you repeat a phrase too often, young people quit hearing it. You can avoid this by using specific, descriptive comments. You may want to steer clear of words that assign a value and get overused, such as *terrific*, *wonderful*, or *fantastic*.

Don't Overdo It

Though verbal praise is an effective reward, high schoolers generally do not like to be singled out in front of their peers. They get embarrassed. Some young people find it difficult to take any kind of direct positive reinforcement. Others are concerned about appearing to be a "teacher's pet." You might want to try praising these group members after a meeting or privately. Writing notes is another great way to offer positive feedback. Be creative! If you do want to recognize someone's good deed before the entire group, do it in a humorous way. Don't be "gushy" or overdo it. While flowery, emotional praise may embarrass your students, calm, quiet, matter-of-fact statements can be effective in giving young people the recognition they need.

In interactions among adults, it is common to pause after making a positive comment, and allow that person to respond. However, using this same interaction pattern with a student in a youth meeting with others watching can cause problems. For example, you might say, "Allison, I thought you made some thought-provoking comments during our small group discussion tonight." But if you point out that she has done a particularly nice job and then pause, she will feel she must respond and may react with a wisecrack or embarrassment. If your praise is always followed by a pause, your comments may cause your students to feel awkward.

You can eliminate this problem by giving positive feedback and then immediately shifting the focus to another topic or young person. So instead of a long pause after the comment to Allison, you could move on to Jacob and ask, "Hey, Jacob, how was the track meet today?" By shifting the focus away from the student who has been praised, you eliminate the pressure that positive feedback potentially puts on young people. Or, you could just continue talking to Allison but move quickly to another topic: "Allison, I really appreciated your comments during small-group time tonight. I've been thinking about moving our small-group time to the basement where we won't have as many interruptions. What do you think of that idea?"

Some young people feel uncomfortable with positive feedback because they've had so little. You may wish to meet privately with these kids to discuss ways they can respond to positive comments. Every young person needs to have enough self-worth to accept recognition from someone else. In the same way, some youth leaders don't know how to give praise, simply because they rarely received praise when *they* were teenagers.

"Norman, it's been my conviction for some time that you've lost control of the high-schoolers."

Reprinted from "Amusing Grace" by Ed Koehler. © 1988 Ed Koehler. Used by permission of InterVarsity Press. P.O. Box 1400, Downers Grove IL 60515.

You may encounter a few young people who will misbehave immediately after a positive comment. These young people view themselves as troublemakers. Though they may take pride in having their efforts noticed by a youth leader, they might tend to panic, thinking, "Now, I'm expected to be perfect." That fear can lead such a young person to misbehave, as a way of saying, "I'm the same problem teenager I've always been." Such misbehavior creates a safe environment for these teens. They will need a lot of private feedback to motivate appropriate behavior. Minor misbehavior should not deter you from encouraging and recognizing success in these young people.

Some of your students have had years and years of seeing themselves as losers. It will not be easy for them to give this up. Your affirmation will be threatening, but wanted all the same.

Be Sure Praise Is Deserved

I've stressed the fact that when a young person is overly criticized, he or she will become discouraged. But if a young person is praised too much, it can have an equally bad effect. Lavish praise that is unmerited not only loses its value as a reward and motivator, it is also discouraging. If you praise everything a young person does, regardless of whether it represents real achievement, effort, or progress, you may make her expect praise even when she doesn't deserve it. Constant praise is neither possible nor desirable.

If the youth leader praises behavior that requires no effort, the young person is likely to be embarrassed because he won't feel he deserved the praise. He may feel he is being praised for babyish behavior, or that the youth leader is trying to con him into working hard. But as long as you are sincere, it's better to overpraise than underpraise. This is doubly true if you are trying to teach yourself to take notice of and remark on the effort and progress of your young people.

Remember that effective praise must be sincere; young people can spot phony praise or false flattery in an instant. You should also be careful not to praise behavior you don't really like—if the young person believes you, he may repeat that same action until you wish you'd been more honest. Praise is like icing on a cake—too little, and the cake is unappealing, but too much can be sickening.

The best time for positive praise is when a young person behaves in a way that is more mature than usual. This doesn't mean that only the highest-performing young people get positive feedback. It means every young person who tries to surpass his or her typical performance should get some recognition from the youth leader.

Praising the Total Group

Acknowledging the efforts of your entire group helps establish a sense of cooperation and community among your youth. Group recognition is also a comfortable way for high schoolers to accept praise and take pride in their accomplishments.

Group praise should be used frequently, but it also must be used carefully. Don't include the entire youth group if the entire youth group wasn't involved. Remember: Praise must be earned. You might say something like, "I've noticed that those of you who have been having personal quiet times have had a dramatic increase in sensitivity to others."

On the other hand, you should avoid group praise that specifically excludes one or two individuals. It would be inappropriate to say, "All but two of the members of our youth group worked hard on this project." This does not serve as praise to the ones who worked—it only draws attention to the two who did not. Group praise should focus on the positive while communicating that all young people are expected to do their best.

" I knew it was over when they put the 'Honk if you're horny' sticker on the bus. Or was it the whoopie cushion under the organist? Maybe it was when . . .

Now Ask Yourself

1. Are you on your kids' team or on their backs most of the time? How would your kids see it?

2. Are there any pet phrases you use repeatedly when praising young people? What are they, and what other phrases could you use?

3. Stop and write a brief note to compliment a young person who did something worthy of praise in the past week.

4. Can you think of some funny items you might give out to recognize young people's achievements? (I have given out old record albums that I've gotten at Salvation Army stores, barf bags from airplanes, packets of hand soap from hotels, etc.)

5. At your next youth meeting, praise at least two young people— one publicly and one privately.

Rules, Boundaries, and Limits

Every ministry needs rules. Rules establish boundaries on behavior. They offer a standard that tells us what is acceptable and what is not. Without rules, stated expectations, and boundaries, you have anarchy. But too many rules can deaden a young person's spirit or incite rebellion. Openness may be the key to finding a balance between these extremes.

Young children respond to power and authority. Teens respond to relationships. If you have a good relationship with your teens they will be more likely to respect your rules. But rules without relationships can lead to rebellion.

Jesus understood rules as a way to encourage his followers into right relationships with God and one another. Rules were intended to help people, not hinder them. For example, he looked at the rules about honoring the Sabbath as a blessing not a burden to people (Mark 2:27-28). Those rules were intended to encourage people to take a restful break from the normal activities of their week.

In Jesus' day, different rabbis had different sets of rules that represented their interpretation of how to live the Torah. Those rules were called the rabbi's "yoke," and when you followed a rabbi, you were taking up that rabbi's yoke. Jesus said in Matthew 11:29-30, "Take my yoke upon you and learn from me, for I am gentle and humble in heart, and you will find rest for your souls. For my yoke is easy and my burden is light."

So how can we follow Jesus by establishing rules that are a blessing rather than a burden to the students in our care? What principles should we use in establishing rules for our ministries? Here are a few "rules about rules" I've found helpful in my own work with youth.

Involve Kids in Setting the Rules

Young people should be encouraged to participate in the rule-making process. We may get kids to obey us for a time by operating from a position of unquestionable authority, but it won't be as healthy or long lasting. It's so easy for us leaders to fall into the myopic trap of believing we have all the answers, but your students have a lot to contribute, too. Teenagers are attempting to gain independence and autonomy, and enlisting their help in designing rules will help them mature and develop self-discipline.

It's good to let the adult leaders and the teens work together to establish rules and guidelines. Encourage both students and adults to share their expectations and try to arrive at a compromise. Although this can be a difficult and frustrating process, it's worth it—because it lets the young people know the leaders have confidence in them. Once the guidelines are established, they need to be posted so everyone is aware of them.

Have the youth group engage in a time of brainstorming to determine some of the rules. The technique of brainstorming was developed by Dr. Alex Osborn, who first applied it to generating ideas to solve problems in business. Osborn pointed out that when people sit down to solve a problem, someone will come up with an idea, and someone else will say, "No, that won't work, because…" This sequence of idea and rebuttal will take place a number of times. The net effect is to inhibit people from coming up with new ideas.

So the first rule of brainstorming is that nobody is allowed to criticize anybody else's ideas. There are no limits on the ideas that may be proposed. Even though some ideas may be impractical, they may stimulate different ideas that will work.

Explain to your youth that you are going to brainstorm some possible rules for the group. Then invite the group members to suggest as many ideas as they can think of, while a note taker writes them all down. There is no particular time limit on this, but you'll normally want to allow anywhere from 5 to 20 minutes. Remember that no one is to critique any of the ideas at this point. You may want to build your rules brainstorming session around these questions: What damages or tears down relationships in our youth group? What builds or fosters relationships in our youth group? You may want to encourage adults to wait until the youth have finished their brainstorming before adding their own ideas. Students will likely name some of the issues adults want to raise.

Once the group is done suggesting ideas, go over them one by one to try to find one or more solutions to a particular problem. The goal is to find solutions the entire group can agree to and feel good about. For this reason, I don't recommend voting on the rules, because voting means someone wins and someone else loses. Obviously, the young people should not be given sole responsibility for determining the group's rules, but it's important to involve them in the process. Young people will be much more inclined to carry out the rules when they are involved in creating them rather than having the rules imposed on them by the youth group leaders. This process also helps reduce hostility on the part of the young people. Since they have agreed to the rules, they are less likely to walk away angry, secretly resolving to sabotage the group's rules.

Most young people develop rules much more demanding than those imposed by adults. And when the young people help make the rules they are much more likely to be enforced, interpreted, and supported. In fact, teens will often set a harsher discipline for themselves than you would, and they will learn from the experience of setting their own boundaries.

Here is a composite list of rules that young people and adult leaders have drawn:

1. Do unto others as you would have them do unto you.
2. When we go on activities, all students ride the church bus or church vans. No student is allowed to drive.
3. All students are to go to class for their grade on youth nights and not change classes.
4. All students attending church activities are expected to participate in that activity and not "hang around" outside the church building.

5. When we return from an activity, parents are to pick up their high schoolers at the time stated.
6. Any youth activities that are planned by students, parents, or teachers that appear to be sponsored by our church must be cleared with the youth minister.
7. Graduation takes place in June at our church. During the summer the graduating seniors are to attend the college activities only.
8. When groups go to Mexico to distribute food and clothing, no one is allowed to purchase fireworks or any illegal materials.
9. In the worship service, we expect our students to have an attitude of respect and reverence. No food or drinks are to be brought into the auditorium during worship service. All hats are to be taken off during the worship service.
10. Students are to turn off all electronic devices during youth meetings.
11. If any student wants to counsel at a camp, they must also attend the camp designed for their age group as a camper.
12. Abstain from wrestling in any of the church buildings. God wants you to use your energy more constructively (or at least outside).
13. Abstain from throwing objects. God doesn't want you to tear a rotator cuff by heaving a projectile across the room. It is not God's will that you knock someone's face off at youth group.
14. Listen to all adult leaders at all times. Praise God for sending these "angels" to look out for your best interests. When they speak, listen.
15. Abstain from any kissing, affectionate hugging, hand-holding, etc., during youth activities. We want you to concentrate on the Lord and this youth group while attending church-sponsored events. No making out allowed.
16. Take care of all church property (games, walls, books, vans, etc.). If you break the church property (thus, the Lord's property) while messing around, expect to fix it or buy a new one.
17. In conversations, if you disagree with someone, criticize the idea—don't attack the person.

18. No whining.

19. One person speaks at a time.

20. Adult sponsors have the final say in the kind of music played and listened to at youth activities.

21. What is said here, stays here. The exception is when an adult needs to seek help for a teen in danger.

22. We solve conflicts through discussion.

23. Show respect for others by not using putdowns. Laugh *with* people, not *at* them.

24. Keep hands and feet to yourselves.

25. No alcohol, cigarettes, drugs, pornography, chew, or cigars at youth activities.

26. Use appropriate language. No cussing, swear words, or profanity.

27. Have fun in the church facilities. Rules are made for our benefit, not to hinder our fun!

Keep Rules to a Minimum

As you think about rules for your group, you might want to take the rules that have been proposed and categorize them all in three groups:

- Rules necessary for youth group preservation
- Rules that would be nice to have
- Rules about things you wish kids would do

After you've placed every proposed rule in one of these categories, throw out the rules you've placed in the "nice" and "wish" categories, and enforce only the "necessary" ones. Those are the key rules for your group.

Keep in mind you don't have to come up with a long list of rules that covers every possible activity. You can have some general guidelines for behavior, as well as specific rules to deal with particular activities. If you are going on a trip, then explain traveling rules. If you will be in a classroom, then explain the rules related to classroom behavior. If you are at a camp, then explain the rules related to a camp setting. I suggest limiting the number of consistent, reasonable rules for any one activity to no more than 10.

Don't set more rules than you are prepared to enforce—that will only cause you heartache. Despite the old saying, good rules are not made to be broken. Good rules are made to be kept.

Rules are like winter clothing. If you put them on all at once, especially before it is necessary, you can smother. Just as it's easy to make a young person frustrated from too many layers of unnecessary clothing, it's easy to pile on too many unnecessary rules.

The more rules and orders you have, the more your young people will disobey. This is not just a matter of arithmetic. We all have a fundamental drive to want to do things for ourselves in our own way. Young people have an inborn, life-giving aggressiveness that makes them fight to overcome obstacles. They seem to know that sooner or later they must stand on their own feet and they need the experience of trying things out themselves while you are there to help them if they fall. But if you are always the obstacle, if you block their plans and direct their every move, if you make rules to cover all contingencies, they either forget the rules or rebel against them.

To be effective, rules must be:
- Simple. Young people must be able to repeat rules and understand them.
- Firm. Rules are not bent by a flimsy excuse.
- Fair. Rules are applied equally to all young people.
- Flexible. Rules can be adjusted occasionally to fit the circumstances.

My friend Doug Miller at Lakeside Church in Folsom, California, has honed all his rules down to three that he posts in his youth facility:
1. Respect Buildings (whatever building you are in, on the church campus or on a trip)
2. Respect Adults (any adult on the church campus or on a trip)
3. Respect Others (anyone or anyone's stuff on the church campus or on a trip)

Make Sure Rules Are Fair and Reasonable

We must make sure our expectations about our students' behavior are realistic and age-appropriate. Expecting a group of junior highers to sit in a classroom for two hours with their hands in their laps and their lips tightly zipped is simply unrealistic. In *The Exuberant Years*, author Ginny Ward Holderness admits that "junior highers are noisy, restless, and mischievous. There are bound to be problems." David Shaheen agrees. "Their preoccupation with self can cause several mood changes within a short period of time," Shaheen writes in *Growing a Junior High Ministry*. "There is no predictable pattern to the way they feel. The same person can be loud and rowdy, or quiet and shy, in a matter of minutes."

In addition to kids' high energy level and moodiness, there's the problem of differing levels of maturity among kids of the same age. There can be as much as a six-year difference in the maturity level of kids in the same grade. With these considerations in mind, we need to develop practical, realistic expectations for behavior. We have to differentiate between behavior that simply irritates us and behavior that truly hurts either the individual or the group.

It's not practical or helpful to make rules our young people are not physically or mentally able to obey. When people feel incapable of carrying out the tasks set before them, they feel lost and small and helpless— perhaps even panicky and embittered. "I'm incapable, so what's the use?" Anyone who has tried to do a job that is too difficult knows this feeling all too well. Don't burden your young people with unreasonable rules that make them feel this way.

The best rules take into account the skills, needs, backgrounds, ages, and personalities of the various individuals in your group, as well as the special personality of the group as a whole. In establishing rules for your group, it is also important to consider the purpose of the group and the need for rules that are enforced consistently and uniformly.

Here are some questions to ask yourself to help determine which rules are fair and necessary for your group and which are not.

1. Is this rule important or is it just a personal preference? In other words, does the rule reflect your ministry priorities or does it merely reflect your personal biases?
2. Will this rule help or hinder your relationships with the students

and their relationships with one another?

3. Will the rule help your young people mature as whole people? Consider how the rule affects the mental, social, physical, and spiritual areas of the students' lives.

4. Is the rule appropriate for your kids? Understanding where your students are developmentally and socially, can you reasonably expect them to follow this rule? Is it consistent and within their ability to obey?

5. Is the rule specific and clearly stated? In other words, do the young people understand what you really mean and what the limits are?

While young people should have a voice in setting the rules that apply to the group, they should all be expected to follow the rules that are established. The young people should not decide whether the rules, once established, should be enforced. If students choose to disobey the rules, they must accept the consequences of that choice.

State Rules Positively

By stating rules in positive terms we focus on behavior that is desired rather than behavior that is unacceptable. A positively stated rule implies to young people that you expect them to function in a mature and responsible way. Avoid overusing the word *don't* when stating rules; a rule that specifically addresses a negative behavior tends to communicate a negative expectation. "Don't talk while someone else is talking," tends to imply, "I expect that you'll be rude and interrupt people."

One big problem with negatively stated rules is that they can quickly grow unmanageable, because the potential list of misbehaviors is virtually endless. Massive "don't" lists make it difficult to respond consistently to misbehavior. I always thought it was ironic that the director of one summer camp our kids attended would always stand up to welcome new campers on the first day, and he'd begin with a long list of all the things they weren't allowed to do. After about 15 minutes worth of don'ts, he'd close with, "But have a great time at camp." The same expectations about behavior can usually be stated in a positive way—simply describe appropriate behavior rather than inappropriate behavior. Young people need to know what they can do as well as what they can't.

Make your communication as positive as possible. It's easy to get into the habit of starting sentences with phrases like…

- "I wish you wouldn't…"
- "Do you really have to…"
- "Isn't there any other way…"
- "Must you…"

Words like these set young people up to feel defensive. On the other hand positively stated rules set out your expectation that your student will behave well. Positively stated rules inform young people that they are with a youth leader who expects their best—and who believes they will give their best.

Make sure everyone understands your expectations about how they are to conduct themselves. It's important to clarify expectations as soon as possible after the new freshmen are brought into your group, because that allows you to make sure rules are understood prior to any opportunities for misbehavior.

Be Specific

If a rule is well defined, a young person knows immediately when it is broken. Youth leaders often assume their young people know what is expected without clearly defining the standards. Many an adult leader has been heard to say, "Well, he should have known that's what I meant." Young people are no better at mind reading than youth leaders are.

If you want things done in a specific way, then give specific instructions. If it doesn't matter exactly how things are done (as long as they get done), then you need not be specific.

In making rules, define what is important and stress it. At the same time, decide what is unimportant and ignore it. Too many adult youth leaders exhaust themselves and wear out their relationships with young people because they spend far too much time and energy focusing on minor issues.

In describing how you want young people to behave, provide as much detailed information as possible. Young people have had many youth leaders and authority figures over the years. Some allow talking; others do not. Some youth leaders want students to raise their hands; others do not. Some let them bring electronic devices on activities; others do not. Each leader must clarify his or her expectations.

In an effort to control his youth group,
Youth Pastor Steve takes some liberties

Make sure students understand how you want them to interact with you and with one another. When leading an activity, make sure your young people know whether they may talk to one another and, if so, how loudly, about what topics, and for how long. Some students will talk through your entire Bible study if they are told only that talking is allowed. It is important to clarify exactly what you mean.

Suppose you say, "I would appreciate it if you would be back to the van at 9:00 tonight." Are your young people likely to believe they *must* be back to the van at 9:00, or just that you'd show appreciation if they came back at 9:00? Be clear and specific in your communication. Major youth group blowups often are the result of unclear communication or guidelines that are too vague.

Communicate your expectations in a firm and resolute voice that lets kids know that you mean what you say. Use words that make clear not only what you want them to do but when you want them to do it (now, never, always). The fewer words you use the better. Extra words cause blank stares, angry confrontations, misunderstood directions, and a host of other problems.

A major difference between the most effective youth leaders and those who are less effective is the degree to which they have defined and communicated their expectations of young people. Effective leaders know how they want students to behave and what they hope to accomplish during every activity. Identify the types of activity included in your ministry, and then design rules and expectations on the basis of this list.

Young people cannot be self-disciplined if they do not know what is acceptable and what is not acceptable. Clear expectations will allow you to respond consistently to behavior, and will give young people a chance to demonstrate their willingness to cooperate.

Dr. James Dobson in *Dare to Discipline* gives an example of a teenager whose mother's *no* meant *maybe*, and how these unclear expectations can cause difficulties:

> Betty Sue is an argumentative teenager. She never takes "no" for an answer. She is very cantankerous; in fact, her father says the only time she is ever homesick is when she is at home. Whenever her mother is not sure about whether she wants to let Betty go to a party or a ball game, she will first tell her she *can't* go. By saying an initial "no," Betty's mom doesn't commit herself to a "yes" before she's had a chance to think it over. She can always change her mind from negative to positive, but it is difficult to go the other way. However, what does this system tell Betty? She can see that "no" really means "maybe." The harder she argues and complains, the more likely she is to obtain the desired "yes."

Many youth workers make the same mistake as Betty Sue's mother. They allow themselves to be swayed when group members whine, argue, or beg. Be sure to think through the stand you want to take on an issue, and then stick with it.

Being specific is also important because young people have a remarkable capacity for finding loopholes and getting around the rules adult leaders impose. "No talking" is answered with "We're not talking—we're whispering." If the youth leader points out that whispering is "just quiet talking," the young people may say, "Why can't we whisper? We're not bothering anybody." The end result is a long dialogue that ends up disrupting the entire group—because now everybody is "talking."

Lee Strobel sometimes uses this example:

I pretend that my daughter, Alison, and her boyfriend are going out for a Coke on a school night and I say to her: "You must be home before 11:00." How would you interpret that? It's pretty straightforward, isn't it?

This would never happen, but suppose it gets to be 10:45 and the two of them are still having a great time at Portillo's Hot Dog Stand. They aren't really anxious to end the evening, so suddenly they begin to have difficulty interpreting my instructions.

They say, "What did he really mean when he said, 'You must be home before 11:00'? Did he literally mean *us*, or was he talking about *you* in a general sense, like people in general? Was he saying, in effect, 'As a general rule, people must be home before 11:00'? Or was he just making the observation that, 'Generally, people are in their homes before 11:00'? I mean, he wasn't very clear, was he?

"And what did he mean by, 'You *must* be home before 11:00'? Would a loving father be so adamant and inflexible? He probably means it as a suggestion. I know he loves me, so isn't it implicit that he wants me to have a good time? And if I am having fun, then he wouldn't want me to end the evening so soon.

"And what did he mean by, 'You must be *home* before 11:00'? He didn't specify whose home. It could be anybody's home. Maybe he meant it figuratively. Remember the old saying,

'Home is where the heart is'? My heart is here at Portillo's, so doesn't that mean I'm already home?

"And what did he really mean when he said, 'You must be home before *11:00*'? Did he mean that in an exact, literal sense? Besides, he never specified 11 p.m. or 11 a.m., and he wasn't really clear on whether he was talking about Central Standard Time or Pacific Time. I mean, it's only quarter to seven in Honolulu. And, as a matter of fact, when you think about it, it's always before 11. Whatever time it is, it's always before the next 11. So with all of these ambiguities, we can't really be sure what he meant at all. If he can't make himself clear, we certainly can't be held responsible."

When Rules Need to Be Changed

Your rules should serve your group—not the other way around. Sometimes you will find that a change in the group's rules or their enforcement would benefit the total group. Don't be afraid to change the rules when conditions change.

At one time our youth ministry had a rule allowing high schoolers to drive their cars to and from activities away from the church if they had proven to be responsible drivers. Eventually, we decided as a group that this rule needed to be changed for two reasons:

1. It was difficult to determine which students were responsible drivers, and the question prompted a number of heated conversations.
2. Our group began to stay in cliques because kids wanted to drive or ride with their friends. Those who were not close to someone who drove and had to ride in the church vans felt like losers.

For the sake of unity and safety, we decided it was important for everyone to ride in a church bus or van. Even though some of the older kids enjoyed being able to drive, they understood the problem with the current situation, so they agreed to change the rule.

It is reasonable to relax rules as young people mature and become more responsible. All rules should be examined carefully from time to time—and those that are unnecessary should be dropped.

Now Ask Yourself

1. Place a mark on the line showing how much involvement your students have in rule making.

A little _____ A lot

2. Enlist your young people's help in designing rules. What are their opinions about the rules you now have? What changes do they want to make?

3. State positively, in writing, the rules you have for your youth group and list the reasons for them. Are there any that are unnecessary? Are there some that need to be changed?

"I like being a youth pastor. I really do. It's just that... well, every once in a while I'd like to run over the junior high group with a steamroller."

Consequences: Natural and Logical

If we want our rules to have weight with our young people, then it's essential that there be consequences for breaking them. It's not always easy to enforce consequences, but it must be done.

This was clear to me several years ago when our traveling youth choir was on tour. A visitor came to me and reported that he'd heard two choir members telling derogatory racial jokes while they were changing clothes in the men's restroom before the concert. Our guest was deeply offended, and left before the concert began.

I confronted the two boys, hoping they would be sorry for what had happened. They were not. In fact, they saw no problem in putting people down in a joking manner—no matter whom it offended. They felt that, if this person couldn't handle the joke, it was *his* problem—not theirs.

Needless to say, I was greatly disappointed by their response. I told them they'd have to spend the next day helping adult volunteers wash choir outfits at a local laundromat, while the rest of the youth choir went to an amusement park.

The boys knew what was expected of them. Before the tour, we'd gone over the rules and the consequences for violating them. These two choir members were not thrilled with me for taking away their trip to the amusement park (in fact, they were angry), but they knew I'd played fair with them. Enforcing rules won't win you popularity contests, but rules are worthless unless there are real consequences for crossing the line.

Although you don't want to reel off a long list of don'ts before each activity, it is important to review rules and consequences. If young people have no idea how you will respond to misbehavior, they will test you to find out. When this happens, you are forced to invent a consequence on the spot, or else overlook the misbehavior. If you implement a consequence that feels unreasonable to the youth, they may feel, justifiably, they've not been treated fairly. If you fail to respond, your young people get the message that such misbehavior is acceptable. It is obviously far better to discuss the consequences for certain behavior and be consistent in following through.

Carrying Out Consequences

Your discipline techniques must show your young people that certain behavior will not be tolerated. At the same time, if your discipline severely embarrasses a student, this can destroy any possibility of your having a positive relationship with that young person. A kid who has felt humiliated by a youth leader is unlikely to do well for that leader again; he will do no more than the bare minimum required to avoid further humiliation.

It is important to remain as calm as possible when following through on discipline. Your staying in control lets the young person know power is not gained through misbehavior.

Like nearly every youth leader, I can overreact to misbehavior when I am tired. When we are physically or emotionally exhausted, it's easy to "lose our cool" or "go off the deep end." I recall one particular time when my overreaction really backfired. There was a certain young man who would come into our high school Sunday school class about halfway through the meeting, look around the room for about three minutes, and then leave. This happened three Sundays in a row. It bothered me that this person refused to join us, and I meant to talk to him about it—but I hadn't had the chance.

On the fourth Sunday I was feeling rushed and underprepared. When the same young person walked into the room halfway through my lesson, I let him have it with both barrels—giving him a piece of my mind I couldn't afford to lose. Even I was surprised by how angry I got. The boy kept trying to say something, but I wouldn't let him get a word in edgewise. Finally, he blurted out, "I'm not in this class! My job is to come in each week and take attendance."

Boy, did I feel dumb and embarrassed! The rest of the kids looked at me and then back at him. Fortunately, this boy was more together than I was. He accepted my apology, and when I started to laugh at how silly I must have looked, he joined in. Soon the entire class was laughing—and I had learned a lesson about staying calm and not jumping to conclusions.

Warn Only Once

Youth leaders should establish definite policies for rule violations and make sure the young people know them. Offer one warning, but only one; if the warning doesn't stop the misbehavior, then be sure to follow through; otherwise, it will be a battle of wills. If the misbehavior continues, the next step in the process involves bringing the offender to a higher authority—such as the head of the youth ministry or a church board official. If the behavior continues, then you may need to call the student's parents. Always approach the young person before you contact parents, and explain what will happen if he or she doesn't straighten out. If a serious situation comes up where the parents must be notified, I usually try to give the young person a chance to explain the situation to the parents first. I will give her a few days to do this—but if she doesn't break the news to Mom and Dad, I expect the student to join me for my talk with the parents.

The key is to deal with problems as quickly and quietly as possible. Use the lowest level of control necessary to eliminate the problem. If you have a tendency to overreact, don't give in to it.

Natural and Logical Consequences

Adult life is structured along the lines of natural and logical consequences. Too many traffic tickets lead to a high insurance premium (logical consequences). Poor personal hygiene leads to poor personal health (natural consequences). With natural consequences there is a built-in outcome that happens without your intervention. In logical consequences the result is determined by an authority figure.

Dr. Rudolpf Dreikurs is usually credited with popularizing the concept of logical consequences. The term *logical consequences* gets its name from a logical relationship between an action and the consequence that follows. Think of it as an "if/then" relationship. "If you don't stay in your tent after lights out, then you won't be permitted to go on future camping trips." Logical consequences can also have a positive result. "If you continue to work hard, then you'll be given more responsibility." Many things in our adult lives operate by standards of logical consequences, and it's vital for youth to learn to deal with such situations if they want to be successful.

The basic principle of natural consequences is to let young people learn from experience wherever possible, as long as it cannot possibly result in serious injury. It's simply letting nature run its course. If a kid eats too much candy, he'll get sick—that's a natural consequence. If the natural consequences of an action are pleasant, the young person will continue to act that way. If the natural consequences are unpleasant, the young person will be motivated to change his actions.

It can be tempting to protect our young people from all unpleasant natural consequences. But if we always protect them, they may not be motivated to change. They need to learn to take care of themselves. By allowing them to learn from natural consequences, we boost their self-confidence and self-esteem.

Becky was responsible for publicity in our youth group. We had planned an important event that we hoped would attract a lot of kids. But Becky completed only half the publicity, and left the rest unfinished with a note on my desk. She was hoping I would finish it.

I called her home and left a message with her mother, explaining that the publicity was Becky's responsibility—if she didn't do it, it wouldn't get done. Becky didn't complete it, and we had only half the number of kids we'd been expecting at our event.

The following Monday, Becky came into my office. She felt like she had let down the whole group. I asked her what she thought she should do next. "Maybe I should just quit," she responded.

"Quit? Why would you quit?" I replied.

"Well, maybe I shouldn't quit," she said. We went on to talk about responsibility and commitment. Becky saw ways she could change her priorities and schedule in order to get things done. We prayed together that God would use her. From that day on, she was a dynamite publicity chairperson. I could always count on her.

Becky is now an active leader in a large church in Nevada; her husband is one of the church's pastors. Becky learned by being allowed to fail and experience the consequences of the failure.

Letting young people experience the consequences of some of their behavior helps them learn to be more responsible. Young people who are protected from the consequences of their bad choices learn the hard way as adults that poor choices result in pain and suffering. But in adulthood, there is often more at stake and the pain is even greater.

Talking It Over

Discussing problems with young people after they have occurred can sometimes help reduce future misbehavior. These conversations can help young people recognize they have control over their actions—that there are many different ways to respond to any given situation.

Arrange to discuss the problem when you and the young person involved are calm. This generally requires a cooling-off period. It's often good to discuss inappropriate behavior the day after it happens. If you interrupt what you are doing and discuss the problem immediately, that may encourage some young people to continue misbehaving because it has forced you to stop teaching and interact with them. Delaying the discussion for a limited time reduces the likelihood of this problem.

If the problem is with a single individual or a very small group of young people, arrange to have your discussion only with those involved in the problem. Select a time and neutral location where no other teens are present—such as a fast-food restaurant at a time when it isn't busy. But if the problem involves a larger number of students, hold your discussion with the entire group. The problem becomes an issue for the whole group if it involves more than a handful of young people.

Plan out what you want to say before you meet with your young people. Begin by explaining how you perceive the problem. Give the young people an opportunity to explain the problem as they see it. Do not allow the discussion to degenerate into a session of accusations and denials. Establish the basic events that led to the problem and what happened.

Let the young people involved know you still care for them even though you don't care for their actions. It is necessary to separate the *deed* from the *doer*. Let them know you'll contact their parents if the misbehavior continues. Help young people to explore other ways of dealing with a similar situation. Young people frequently know only one way to respond to a situation. End the discussion by communicating a positive expectation of future behavior.

Involving Parents

If parents are supportive and interested, parental contacts can be a useful strategy for eliminating behavior problems. But these contacts are important even if the parents are not supportive, or seem to have little impact on the young person's behavior.

Parents have a right to know if there are problems with their kids in the church, and you have the right to assistance from parents. By working together you can solve many disruptive behaviors before they escalate into major problems.

We had a girl who decided to sneak away from a youth meeting and go do some drinking with a friend. When she came back, our adult volunteers could smell the liquor on her breath. The sponsors talked to her but decided not to tell her parents. In hindsight I can now see we probably should have informed the girl's parents, even though it would have been painful for all those involved. Her parents are terrific people and would have handled the situation maturely. Instead, we decided to play parent and handle it ourselves. Later, the girl's parents did find out about the incident—and were greatly disappointed that we'd not informed them of the situation.

When speaking to parents, state clearly and firmly the problem the young person is having. Tell the parents you need their support. When you contact a parent regarding a problem, and that parent supports your efforts, take the time to show your appreciation by sending a note or making a quick call.

Parents need to know your expectations in order to support you. You may want to send home a letter each year to the parents of all incoming group members, outlining your discipline plan. This can help parents become your allies during any flare-ups.

Parents are accustomed to receiving only negative news when an adult youth leader contacts them. Be sure to send home a positive note when you notice improved behavior. This communicates that you have a positive attitude toward their son or daughter and will increase your chances of gaining their support if there is a problem.

When problems do arise, document them. Keep detailed records of inappropriate behavior. Doing so will enable you to relate problems in a fair, nonjudgmental manner to parents.

One school principal discovered by accident an effective way to discipline problem junior highers. "A kid came into my office whom I had talked to a number of times for minor discipline problems—talking in class, being late, not bringing materials, driving the teachers crazy," relates John Lazores of Wilson Junior High in Hamilton, Ohio. At one point Principal Lazores got fed up and said, "The next time I see you, we're going to have your mother come in and see what we have to put up with all day." The young person's reaction was, "Do anything you want, but don't have my mother come in."

But his mother did come in—and spent a full day in class. Since then about 60 parents have put in their time at Wilson. Results? Detentions are down from 20 per day to none on some days; expulsions have dropped from 120 per year to only 11 in the year since the new program began. Said Lazores, "Kids who have seen other kids' parents in school stop causing problems because they don't want their own parents to sit with them all day."

But punishment is only one aspect of the parental involvement at the school. "In education, we're only as effective as the parents," says Lazores, "and now we have parents who can call us once a week to check up on the kids' progress." The net result has been improved grades and behavior by kids, and greater involvement by parents.

Contracting

Most church youth workers are unfamiliar with the term *contracting* as applied to relationships between adult leaders and youth. We're all aware that, in the world of business, a contract represents an agreement between two parties. Party A promises to do something, and party B promises to do something in return.

As a discipline method in the youth group, contracting uses exactly the same concept. The contract is a positive way of disciplining young people that involves the leader and the youth negotiating an agreement that includes a commitment from both sides.

Although a contract between a young person and the adult leader can be purely verbal, there are several advantages to having a formal written contract. A written agreement can prevent misunderstanding and arguments. It also emphasizes the responsibilities of both the adult leader and the young person in relation to their respective parts of the contract.

A good contract should include the following:
1. A brief overall statement of the goal
2. What the young person should do, rather than what she should not do
3. Specific language that avoids vague, unclear terms
4. How behavior will be evaluated and monitored
5. How long the contract will be in effect
6. The adult youth leader's responsibility

The following page shows an example of a contract made to encourage a student who has been misbehaving in a Sunday school class.

Contract Agreement
Student: Laurie Hanover
Adult youth leader: Jane Cromwell
Specific time: Sunday school hour

Areas Needing Attention	Appropriate Behavior	Inappropriate Behavior
Listening to directions given in meetings	Having eye contact with those giving directions	Talking to friends, using cell phone when directions are being given
Staying in the youth room during meetings	Using the restroom before meetings	Going outside of youth room without obtaining permission
Keeping your hands and feet to yourself	Keep your body in your own space	Pushing, nudging, kicking others

Evaluation: Each week after Sunday school the adult volunteer and the student will get together to evaluate that Sunday's behavior. At the end of five weeks, if there have been no problems, the student will be allowed to participate in the Christmas All-Nighter (or whatever activity fits your group).

_____   _____
Student's signature   Adult volunteer's signature

About Corporal Punishment

Corporal punishment is one form of discipline I don't ever recommend youth workers use, even as a last resort. Corporal punishment involves the use of physical force against someone else. It most commonly involves spanking with an open hand, belt, or paddle, but can also include hitting, ear pulling, and strong-arming.

Corporal punishment has severe drawbacks as a consequence for misbehavior. Corporal punishment can be very demeaning for teens. It goes beyond embarrassment to the point of being humiliating. Such discipline can easily get out of hand when a youth leader is angry or frustrated. Some group members are amused when they can "push an adult youth leader over the edge." Some students even consider it a status symbol—showing how "tough" they are by prompting and enduring physical punishment.

To most teens mild corporal punishment is more of a joke than an effective tool for shaping behavior. I know of one inexperienced Sunday school teacher who sought to use such a method to control an unruly group of ninth-grade boys: When somebody got out of hand, the teacher would bop the student on the head with a foam rubber bat. Of course, it didn't really hurt. Instead of preventing problems, this method caused kids to act like they wanted punishment—and laugh when they got it!

The final compelling drawback against using corporal punishment with teens is that it teaches young people to use physical violence whenever you want someone to behave differently. Corporal punishment implies that the person with the most power or physical strength is the person who is right. Youth groups need to provide a model that teaches young people to work out their problems intelligently rather than by resorting to physical force.

You May Lose a Few

Before we leave the topic of consequences, there is one other consequence you must keep in mind. No matter how hard you try to use a positive approach to discipline and create an environment where all your young people can grow, mature, and have fun, you will lose some young people. Some kids will resist your every attempt to maintain order. Eventually, you may decide you have no choice but to let go of those kids who refuse to behave. I would rather run the risk of losing a few young people who continually refuse to follow the rules rather than face the certainty of damaging them all by not using any discipline.

Learning is impossible in an atmosphere of disorder. Teaching kids to respect God cannot happen if we allow chaos to reign supreme in God's house. A permissive attitude toward group anarchy is the most certain way to guarantee the failure of your objectives.

"I volunteered you as a counselor for the junior high boys' overnight raft trip."

Reverend Feldon gets even with his wife for volunteering him to speak at the women's tea.

Now Ask Yourself

1. Do your young people know the consequences for breaking the rules? If not, how can you let them know in a positive manner?

2. What is the difference between natural and logical consequences?

3. What are some natural consequences you have observed in your youth group over the previous month?

4. Which of these best describes your style of handling problems in your youth group? What are the strengths and weaknesses of your primary approach?

   Deny the problem. "There is nothing wrong with my youth group," or "I don't have any problems."

   Appeal to authority. "In our church we know how to handle young people like that," or "My professor always said to handle young people this way," or "The church board ought to deal with this."

   Minimize the problem. "There's really nothing to worry about. I'll have this straightened out in no time," or "It's a phase they are going through."

   Look for personal satisfaction. "In my youth group these young people had better do what I tell them to do. I don't have the time or energy to put up with any foolishness."

   Be a pure empiricist. "Before I can do anything, I'll need to know the facts and only the facts."

   Be intuitive. "I just know inside that something is wrong."

5. How can you inform/involve parents in the area of discipline with your young people?

6. Do you think spanking and other forms of corporal punishment are effective in curtailing misbehavior at any age? If so, at what age should it cease, and why? Is it appropriate for parents to use corporal punishment? What about youth leaders?

"Our young people are away at their national convention. So far the stats include three conversions, fourteen recommitments, six minor injuries, and two counselor breakdowns."

Anger: Yours and Theirs

It was happening again. As Joe Youth Minister struggled on, trying to teach this week's Sunday school lesson to his class of rowdy ninth-graders, he felt his anger building inside. "Hey, you guys, be quiet!" he said, for what felt like the hundredth time. A trio of especially rambunctious boys in the corner started to laugh.

When Joe turned around to write on the whiteboard, a spitball came flying over his shoulder and splattered on the board, inches from Joe's head. Losing it, Joe spun around and hurled the chalk in the direction of the troublemakers in the corner. "Don't try that again!" he yelled.

Instantly, guilt set in. Once again his attempts at discipline had failed. Once again anger had taken control of Joe and his classroom. He wondered if it was time to get into another line of work.

All youth workers get angry with their kids. And I think it's quite natural and completely acceptable to get angry from time to time. I think we have a false expectation that we should never get angry with kids and that we've failed any time we do. I think the real questions we need to consider are: *What kinds of things make us angry?* and *How do we handle our anger?*

Reasons Leaders Get Angry

Why do youth leaders get so angry with their teenagers? Aren't we supposed to nurture, love, encourage, and lead them? Isn't that why we're in this work in the first place?

The more I think about it, the more I realize that the times when I've been most angry with kids have involved my own bloated expectations.

I'd read Ephesians 3:20 about God's power to do "immeasurably more than all we ask or imagine." Therefore, I expected God would go far beyond my hopes for my students. I thought I couldn't dream big enough for him.

As a result, I was constantly filled with big dreams that ended up on the ash heap. I became angry when the kids didn't perform as I hoped and expected. My anger was often rooted in the frustration that their behavior didn't meet my high hopes.

Our anger can also be related to our own insecurities. Some adult youth leaders who feel insecure go out of their way to prove that they are in control. Afraid that their power is eroding, they're quick to make young people knuckle under—and grow extremely angry if the young people will not give in. If you don't feel secure, try to pinpoint your areas of insecurity and work on them. Don't let insecurity become an excuse for acting rashly or harshly. Teens need adult youth leaders who serve as leaders and counselors, not as overlords.

Reasons Jesus Got Angry

We might be tempted to think that Jesus never got angry—but that's not what the Bible teaches. If Jesus is our model, the kinds of things that made him angry should infuriate us as well. As I looked into God's Word, I discovered a couple of things that clearly made Jesus angry:

- **Irreverence.** In John 2:13-22, we read about how Jesus drove the moneychangers out of the temple. He was incensed by the irreverent use of God's house as a flea market.
- **Hypocrisy.** When Jesus was about to heal the man with the withered hand (Mark 3:1-6), the Pharisees condemned him for healing on the Sabbath. In this case, their hypocrisy and lack of compassion aroused his wrath.

I think we youth leaders who take Jesus as our model have a right—even a responsibility—to confront teenagers who are irreverent and hypocritical. But I think we need to be somewhat cautious about this. We must remember that when Jesus got angry with someone, we can trust that his perception and insights were correct. We know ours are flawed. So I don't want to give every youth worker the absolute green light to vent our anger toward any kid we feel is acting irreverent, just because "that's what Jesus would do." Maybe that is what Jesus would do, but it's impossible for us to know exactly how Jesus would respond to that kid, with that background, and in that situation. Remember that the Bible says, "In your anger do not sin" (Ephesians 4:26). That's the challenge. When we express our anger, we need to avoid becoming violent, insulting, profane, or degrading.

"The junior highers say that they're really sorry and it won't happen again"

Dealing Constructively with Our Anger

So how do leaders deal constructively with anger? I think we need to begin by accepting graciously that anger is here to stay. A hundred thousand adult youth leaders cannot be wrong; we've all been angry with our young people at times. Our anger has a purpose; it shows our concern. Failure to get angry in certain situations would show indifference, not love. Those who love cannot avoid anger. This doesn't mean our young people should be forced to withstand torrents of rage and floods of violence. But it does mean they can benefit from anger that says, "Enough is enough, there are limits to my tolerance."

When we are feeling angry and irritated inside, but continue to be serene and complacent on the outside, we convey hypocrisy—not kindness. Instead of trying to hide our irritation, we need to learn how to express it effectively. Anger, like a deep breath, cannot be held indefinitely. If we keep trying to hold it all in, sooner or later, we are bound to explode. And when we lose our temper, it's almost as if we become temporarily insane. We attack and insult. We say and do things we normally wouldn't do, hurting those we love. When the battle is over, we feel guilty and resolve never again to lose our temper. But anger soon strikes again.

When feelings of anger are constantly stifled, both physical and mental health deteriorates. Anger has an energy that must find an outlet. If we deny ourselves an outlet, that energy starts to consume us. Instead of trying to suppress anger, find ways to express it in nondestructive ways. The best expressions of anger can bring some relief to you as well as insight to your teenager—with no harmful aftereffects for either. As we express anger, we should consciously seek to avoid creating waves of resentment and revenge. We want to get our point across and then let the storm subside.

Understanding your anger and expressing it in a healthy manner is crucial to your relationship with young people. It is important that you model for teenagers how to handle anger. Try not to blame, attack, or insult someone who has angered you. Instead, try confronting the other person with an "I" statement, such as "Jeff, when you poke other students, I feel upset because I must stop teaching to act as a referee." Such an "I" statement attempts to put the incident into perspective, by describing the upsetting behavior, how it makes you feel, and how it affects you. These statements focus on the disruptive behavior, while helping the young person become more aware of how his behavior affects others.

Another way to release anger and psychological tension is to engage in some physical activity. Next time you are feeling angry, try taking a vigorous walk around the building. That will provide you an opportunity to release some energy and unwind.

On those occasions when you feel the need to explode and "dump" your anger on a young person, do so in writing. Take a few minutes to write to the "offending" person about your angry feelings. Let it all come out. Don't save anything. Let the person know how furious he or she has made you feel. Be emotional; don't try to be logical. Once you have it all out on paper, fold it, address it, and then throw it away. (You might want to tear it up first!) You will be amazed at how successful this technique is in satisfying your need to express anger. Once you've had opportunity to vent your anger in this way, you can then approach the problem more rationally and with less emotion.

Remember there's often a vast difference between God's will for the young people with whom we work and what we hope will happen in their lives. But as we grow more in touch with God's plan, as we focus on his priorities rather than ours, as we learn more about human nature, we'll grow more in tune with God and better able to pick up the melody he is playing in the lives of our young people. Consider these suggestions for dealing with anger:

1. Study the Scriptures. Use the Bible to understand human nature, how God responds to it, and how he transforms sinners to his likeness. When I'm feeling angry at my youth group's uncaring attitude, it helps me to read the book of Jonah and see him express similar feelings. When I'm feeling discouraged and tempted to give up on my students, I appreciate the stories of how people like Moses and Elijah also slipped into the pits of discouragement at times. As I look at how God deals with these people, I am stunned at how often he was patient, kind, and understanding, rather than angry. When we see young people as God sees them—as sheep without a shepherd—we are better able to love them as God does.

2. Find a loyal friend. A friend can help you gain perspective. If your expectations are too high, an objective friend can help you become more realistic. When you are discouraged, a friend can lift you up. Ask God to provide someone in your life that can listen, provide tactful counsel, and help you see as God sees.

3. Strive to understand teenagers. Knowing the psychology of the average teenager can help you understand why your kids seem apathetic or into "all the wrong things." It will also help you keep cool when they do things you don't like.

4. Stick to God's priorities. The longer I'm in youth ministry, the more I see the wisdom of how Jesus poured his life into 12 people. I think we need to do the same as youth pastors. I love it when the church is jammed with kids craning their necks and smiling at a huge rally or concert. But the kids who really last are the ones who get discipled. Jesus made a priority of sharing his life with the Twelve; we need to do the same with the kids in our ministries.

So when you find yourself getting angry at the kids under your leadership, ask yourself these questions:

- Do I understand how God deals with struggling people?
- Are my expectations too high?
- Do I know what makes teenagers tick?
- Are my priorities in order?

When you focus on the things Jesus focused on, you'll tend to get angry at the kinds of things that angered him. But you'll also begin to love as he loved, lead as he led, and give as he gave.

Preventing Molehills from Becoming Mountains

There are times when you'll get angry with your students. That's the nature of this ministry. But here are a few dos and don'ts to help you prevent molehills of frustration from growing into mountains of anger:

Don't...
- Use a sarcastic tone or put kids down.
- Quit.
- Handle the problem in front of the whole group.
- Get into a power struggle.
- Humiliate.
- Ignore bad behavior.
- Be surprised at bad behavior.

- Tell other people about your private confrontation with the person who made you angry.
- Do anything drastic until you listen a lot, think a lot, and pray a lot.
- Allow discussions to turn into destructive arguments.

Do…
- Pause before taking "official action." Always count to 10. Better yet, try 110.
- Admit your anger.
- Ask the person to talk with you privately.
- Speak firmly.
- Make it clear you expect good behavior.
- Call off the activity if you're unable to deal with the bad behavior any other way.
- Enlist other adults for advice, help, prayer, and support.
- Train adults to deal with anger.
- Train adults to move physically close to the person making trouble.
- Confer with parents if you're unable to work out the problem.
- Intervene immediately when violent behavior occurs.
- Notice good behavior and tell the person.
- Cool off briefly before you discuss the problem with the person.
- Be specific about the behavior you object to.
- Apologize if you're wrong.
- Allow the person to save face.
- Demonstrate forgiveness to the person who made you angry.
- Share a prayer of thankfulness when the conflict is over and the problem resolved.
- Ask the person what course of action they think you should follow. (The "misbehaver" often has a good idea that will take care of the situation.)

When Young People Get Angry

Of course, it's not just adults who get angry. As youth workers we're dealing with kids who sometimes struggle to handle their own emotions. It's important to recognize the kinds of things we may do that can anger the young people we work with.

In his book *How We Make Our Kids Angry* (2007), Roger Cross suggests some primary ways adults make teens angry:

- Pressuring teens to be something they are not. Pushing, cajoling, nagging, or "guilting" kids into a particular life direction or career path without considering their wishes or dreams.
- Loving teens for what they do instead of who they are. Raising kids in a performance-based environment.
- Favoring some teens over others. When kids sense disparity, they become hurt and angry.

- Treating teens with disrespect. Violating kids' self-esteem through insults and humiliation.

Children often store up a great deal of anger because they do not have adequate means of releasing feelings of frustration, confusion, and helplessness. Teenagers, however, have greater opportunity and ability to release these charged feelings. The combined force of pent-up anger from the past and current anger sometimes causes teenagers to overreact.

Adolescent anger is often closely associated with the need to rebel or push away from parents and other authority figures. Energy from the anger is used to strengthen the pushing-away process. Angry reactions may also express a young person's need to gain a greater sense of control over her life. Although these emotions can be uncomfortable and often scary to deal with, they can be normal and healthy when handled appropriately. But when such anger is mishandled, it can turn into rage, hostility, or resentment. Rage is anger that is so intense that it is beyond a person's control. Hostility is anger that is felt for a longer period of time and involves the wish or impulse to inflict pain or harm to the object of the anger. Resentment develops when a hurt or transgression is not confronted and forgiven.

Don't try to win an argument with an extremely angry young person. You can't—she will only get angrier. The young person needs to get the anger out before you can reason with her. She needs to get it out in a way that will not cause any damage. Don't let her repress it, or it will simply go underground and build.

Be thankful when a young person trusts you enough to let you see his anger. Try to stay calm as he pours out all his anger. After the anger is out, he will be emotionally drained and more open to your input. Be sure to affirm him by telling him you are proud that he didn't take his anger out in more aggressive ways.

Now Ask Yourself

1. How do you handle anger in your own life? What are some ways you can improve your ability to deal with difficult situations?

2. Make a list of positive ways to dispel anger.

3. How would you handle an extremely angry teenager?

9

Engaging Your Kids and Avoiding Distractions

Susie Youth Worker was puzzled. She'd worked very hard on today's Bible study lesson for the high school group. She knew the topic was relevant to the needs of her students. She had lots of energy and enthusiasm, interesting information, and great visuals. But 15 minutes into the lesson, as she looked out across the dingy basement meeting room, she knew she'd lost her students. Most of them were slouched in their metal folding chairs and had dazed expressions on their faces. A few, clustered in the back corner, were whispering to one another, though the dim light made it hard to tell who was speaking. A feeling of sleepiness and apathy had settled on the warm, quiet room. She even felt her own energy draining away. *Where did I go wrong?* Susie wondered.

Without realizing it, our friend Susie was close to figuring out what was wrong as she looked around the room. In this case the problem was centered on the atmosphere rather than the content or presentation. Many discipline problems can be headed off at the pass if we stop to consider how the physical environment affects learning and behavior.

Consider Your Environment

Be sure to consider the room used by your young people. Do all you can to allow students to make that room their own. Involve them in decorating the space. If your budget permits, you might have them paint the room or put in new carpet.

Each week or month put new posters or enlarged photos on the walls. All young people will get distracted from time to time during a lesson, and they'll often look around the room as their minds may begin to wander. The secret is to have things on the walls that relate to the topic of the day. Even if they do look around, they will still be getting the thrust of your message through other visual methods.

Church rooms are often overheated, especially during the winter. Heat tends to make us sleepy and contributes to the lethargy some teenagers experience naturally. You can alleviate the situation by opening a window or resetting the thermostat. Cleanliness is also important. You don't need a hospital-white sterile room, but you want your young people to be proud of the room where they meet. Make sure the room is well ventilated, and not full of clutter.

You also want to make sure your room is well lit. Church rooms can have too much or too little light—either of these extremes can create problems. If your room has extremely bright, harsh lighting, you can simply turn off some of the lights, or if they are on a timer switch, you can unscrew some of them. Bring more lights from home if your room is dim. Good lighting will help young people become more relaxed and receptive to learning.

Room dividers can create a variety of spaces for get-away zones, learning centers, preparation areas for skits, or for discussion groups. The only drawback is that these dividers are not soundproof. With several discussion groups going at the same time in one room, the noise can be unbearable.

Arrange furniture to meet teaching and learning goals. If your goals call for group work, you may want to cluster chairs or tables. Let your learning objectives determine the furniture arrangement rather than allowing the layout of your room to dictate how you teach.

The size of the room and the number of chairs are also important. If you have a large room set up with 500 chairs, and you know you are only going to have 15 young people, you are asking for trouble. When kids come into the room, it looks as though you were planning for a lot more people. They'll feel like they made the wrong choice in coming, because it's obvious that 485 people went somewhere else! No matter what happens in that meeting, your kids will feel like it can't be very good because "no one is here." If you only have four kids in your youth group, don't meet in the main auditorium. You're better off meeting in a closet or restroom! Then, when you get six kids coming, you can move into a larger room (maybe the custodian's office). Cramming into a small room has a great psychological effect on kids, and it's also a lot of fun.

Preparing for Your Meeting

It's very important that you arrive early for youth meetings. When you are there to greet young people at the door, you demonstrate your interest in interacting with them from the moment they arrive. Students feel secure knowing they are in the right room at the right time and that the youth leader is ready for them. Your presence will also reduce the likelihood of misbehavior. If young people enter the room rambunctiously or disruptively, you can take care of the inappropriate behavior prior to the meeting.

You'll also want to make sure you have all your materials ready before the meeting. If you teach middle school students, and you turn away from the class to write on the whiteboard and can't find the marker, you may be in trouble. As you frantically look for that missing pen, the kids will begin to talk to one another, move around the room, throw paper airplanes, stand on their chairs, and do strange dances. It'll take you another 10 minutes to get their attention back—all because you didn't have a marker on hand when you started.

Coping with Late Arrivals

Does it drive you up the wall when half your group walks into the youth meeting just in time for the closing prayer? Kids who arrive late can be very disruptive. Every time a young person comes into the room late, everything stops as everyone else stares at the latecomer. Most of the time these latecomers won't just slip in quietly and find a seat. No, most kids will feel the need to make sure everyone knows they are here now so everything can begin.

Start your meetings on time and with a "bang" to encourage promptness.

Don't run after kids, scream, or remind them what time it is. Instead, start each meeting with a quick, hilarious activity that'll grab their attention. Change the opener each time so kids never know what to expect. Eventually, they'll be hooked on your creativity.

Another way to help eliminate disruptions is to have an adult youth leader posted at the back door so latecomers can be escorted in quietly at an appropriate time in the program.

Showing DVDs and Videotapes

Videos can be a great way to engage your group, but some kids will look for trouble the minute the lights are dimmed. There are several things that can be done to prevent discipline problems from occurring when showing DVDs or videotapess in your youth group.

1. Preview all videos. Don't trust anyone else's opinion of a movie. I once showed my group a film recommended to me by some friends (and I use the term *friends* loosely). They said the film was about two guys who cross the Sahara Desert on motorcycles and become Christians during the journey. Supposedly the two riders were intending to make a secular movie about their journey for a major studio but later decided to make a Christian film out of it. Without previewing it, I showed it to my kids one Sunday evening. It was the worst film I've ever seen.

Imagine these two guys riding what looked like Honda 50s across the desert. The first few minutes of the film featured the two motorcyclists going about 10 miles per hour on a flat, straight stretch of desert. There was no dialogue, only the putt-putt-putt of the bikes. It was so boring I was dying!

It got worse. Evidently the real cyclists had become Christians on the trip, after they'd had an accident and were assisted by two missionaries. Of course, they did not have their cameras rolling when the accident happened, so they had to fake it. Did you ever see the skit from the old television comedy *Laugh-In* where an old man rides a tricycle into a tree and falls over? Well, that's what the accident looked like—these guys gently fell over on their bikes and then smiled into the camera. Two missionaries appear in the desert out of nowhere; he's wearing a suit and she's wearing a dress and high heels. It was incredible. My kids were laughing so hard they were falling on the floor! I stopped the film and never saw how it ended. So much for great moments in youth ministry.

2. Make sure you have access to the DVD or videotape and a player, and that you know how to work the equipment. It can be embarrassing to announce a movie and then be unable to show it for some reason. I have a friend who had to tell 2,300 high school kids who had gathered in an auditorium that he didn't have the film they'd come to see, because he hadn't ordered it in time. Don't let this happen to you.

3. If you want to use a film to illustrate a point in your lesson, you may want to show just a clip instead of an entire movie. Many films are too long for youth meetings. You're better off showing just a scene or two to illustrate biblical truths for your students. You can use a clip to illustrate a point, or build an entire presentation around it.

4. After a particularly moving film, don't rush to turn on all the lights. The kids may be dabbing their tears and feeling embarrassed. Leave the lights out and discuss the film in the quiet darkness.

Don't Bore Kids with the Bible

Jim Rayburn, founder of Young Life, said it many years ago, and we've yet to improve on his insights: "It is a sin to bore kids with the Bible." The Word of God is far too important for us to merely mumble our way through a Bible study in an unprepared manner.

I wouldn't dream of going on a retreat without having every logistical detail covered, but I admit that I've sometimes stood up to speak having done very little preparation. I don't do my best job when I choose to "wing it." I have also noticed an interesting phenomenon: The less prepared I am, the grouchier I get.

One of the great communicators in Scripture (next to Jesus) was Apollos. According to Acts 18:24-28, Apollos was a class A communicator, who knew his stuff and spoke with exactness. Kids need the same from us if they are to see the Word of God as active, sharp, and exciting.

Keeping Students' Attention as You Speak

Always make sure you have everyone's attention before you begin teaching. If you start teaching while some young people are talking or are out of their seats, students will assume it's okay to engage in those behaviors while youth group is in session. Make a habit of waiting until you have everyone's attention before giving directions or starting activities. You may discover that a little time spent eliminating potential distractions will pay off by eliminating the need for some discipline.

Here are some other techniques to help you keep the attention of your group:

- Don't stand in front of a bright window when you are speaking—it makes your facial features almost indistinguishable. Kids need to see you if you want to keep their attention.

- Speak on the level of your kids. Don't talk down to them. They are not children; so don't speak to them as if they were. On the other hand, you should use words that are concrete, descriptive, and familiar. You may have a seminary or college education, but your kids don't. Put the cookies on the lower shelf.

- Use illustrations and stories. The best speaker is the one who turns ears into eyes.

- Use visual aids. For many kids, seeing something once is better than hearing about it 100 times.

- If you say "in closing," you have 60 seconds maximum to wrap up that message.

- Speak and teach with enthusiasm and conviction. The human spirit is attracted to conviction; it's repelled by half-heartedness. Kids who say their youth group is "boring" or "too serious" are often saying the group lacks conviction. Conviction is more than simple belief. It's living passionately for what you believe.

- Get out from behind the podium. You want nothing between you and your audience but words.

- Lean forward a bit as you speak, with one foot slightly in front of the other.

- Use facial expressions.

- Use powerful gestures. Move around the room.
- Speak so they can hear you. Watch speed, tone, and volume.
- Make eye contact. Next to your mouth, your eyes are your greatest tool in communicating.
- Use humor. Students like to laugh.
- Involve your audience. Ask them to do something (raise hands or arms, put hand on chin, cross arms, etc.). Bring an audience member up front.
- Have confidence. Dogs sense fear—and so do teenagers! Confidence is a key to capturing and keeping kids' attention during "serious" activities. But confidence isn't the same as cockiness. Confidence means you're well prepared, secure, humble, and honest. When kids don't want to be serious, your confidence will help draw them in.

Videotape Your Teaching

Tape your times with the kids, especially if you are having difficulty. Place the video recorder in an unobtrusive spot. If the young people ask about it, tell them you are taping the class to improve your teaching.

The recorder should be turned on for the class period. Students will often be less disruptive when the recorder is turned on, which is, of course, one of the added benefits of the technique. But the tape itself will give you a chance to evaluate your own interactions with your youth group.

Cutting Down on Chatter

There are a number of effective techniques for dealing with kids who talk while you are speaking. Here are four I've found helpful:

Stopping Speaking: Sometimes it's best to simply stop speaking until everyone is listening. Even if you're in mid-sentence, just stop. This is a way to let kids know your lesson or activity is important; it shouldn't have to compete with anything else. Usually, if you just stop and wait, the kids will quiet down within a few seconds. If it takes longer, you might say something like, "We'll begin when everyone's ready to listen." If the problem is severe, you might even just pull up a chair and sit down. Inevitably, the kids tell one another to be quiet. It's positive peer pressure. This approach helps kids realize for themselves the inappropriateness of talking when someone else has the floor. By deciding to settle down, they're learning how to act in a group. Kids also learn to police one another—the discomfort of watching a leader silently stare at the group provokes many kids to say, "Shhhhh!" The technique also leaves kids' dignity intact. No one is yelled at or belittled. Your message is: "I respect you as people, but I won't battle you for the right to be heard. You decide if the group would benefit from quieting down."

Silent Speaking: If two or three young people start talking as you are speaking to the group, continue moving your mouth as if you are talking, but don't let any sound come out of your lips. It will get deadly silent in the room as the entire group wonders if they are going deaf! However, the kids who are talking will suddenly sound extremely loud. They will look up, realize everyone hears them, and stop. Then you can continue as usual and no one is particularly embarrassed.

Hand Clapping: When students get too chatty, try the following surefire chat stopper. In a quiet voice, say, "If you hear me, clap once." (Pause to let those who hear you clap). Then say, "If you hear me, clap twice." (Clap-Clap) "If you hear me, clap three times." (Clap-Clap-Clap) Continue until the entire class is quiet and clapping.

Eye Contact: Sometimes all you need to do is make eye contact with a young person who is talking to others. Simply look at the young person as you are talking until you get her attention. Let your eyes communicate that you need her to focus on what you are saying.

Move around the Room

You may have noticed that your rowdy young people tend to sit in the back of the room. Why not simply move to the back of the room and speak from there after everyone is seated? Have all the kids turn their chairs around. The back row becomes the front row. Each time the class meets, speak from another part of the room. Your disruptive kids won't know where to sit because they will not know where you'll be standing as you speak.

"Borrow" Distracting Items

Occasionally young people will bring distracting items to youth meetings. Some of these items include electronic games, hats or balls that are tossed around the room, knives that are being shown off, or someone's pet snake, lizard, or mouse. If you loudly demand that a high schooler "hand that over," the young person may feel pressure to fire back a retaliatory remark. It's far better to ask them to "loan" you the item for the hour or day or week—depending on where you are.

As you confiscate something, focus on the item, not the young person. You may want to make it humorous to ease the tension. Give the item a suspension. Talk to the item and scold it. In confiscating a Nerf football that's been thrown around the room, say, "I can't believe you did that! You've never acted this way before." The kids laugh, the problem is solved, and you can move on to more important things.

Keep Disruptive Kids Busy

If you have a student who cannot sit still, give him something to do. I'm not talking about putting him in a leadership position to straighten him out. That usually backfires. But you can involve disruptive students in activities like passing out or collecting papers. Keep them busy and involved without drawing attention to them, and many times the problem will be solved.

Now Ask Yourself

1. What changes do you need to make in the room where your students meet on a regular basis?

2. Is there another room that would meet your needs better than the room where you now meet?

3. What are some quick engaging activities you could use to start off your meetings?

4. What visual aids could you use in your teaching?

5. What skills and techniques do you need to work on to be a more effective communicator?

"To keep junior highers from swinging from the balcony."

10

Everyday Discipline Challenges

This chapter offers you a smorgasbord of advice—a variety of disciplinary methods to deal with a variety of situations. Feel free to mix and match these approaches to meet the needs of your group.

Be Willing to Say No

Youth workers want to be liked, so it's tempting to be lax when it comes to discipline, especially at first. But the truth is it is much harder to add rules later. It's far better to start off with more control and loosen up a bit later.

The problem many leaders have is saying no to kids. It is probably the most difficult word to say in the English language because so few of us use it. But it's important to remember that Jesus said no to many people in a variety of situations. Archbishop George H. Niederauer of San Francisco, while a faculty member at St. John's Seminary in Camarillo, California, delivered a message titled "When Jesus Said No." He pointed out that Jesus said no to human requests (Matthew 8:21-22; Luke 4:42-44; 10:38-42), to friends requesting favors (Matthew 20:20-23; Mark 8:31-38; Luke 9:54-56; Acts 1:6-7), to the demands of the crowds around him (Matthew 12:38-45; Luke 4:23-24; John 6:41-58), and to common-sense, law-and-order, citizens' requests (Mark 2:18-22; 14:4-9; Luke 9:12-17; 19:37-40). Jesus understood that a life of love for others means we sometimes have to say no. We youth workers have to follow his lead.

"Nope, the kids were no trouble at all."

Recognize Individual Problems

Remember that your entire youth group is never at fault when things go wrong. At times it may seem like everyone is acting up, but in reality, it's usually just two or three young people. If you can control these individuals, you can control the entire group. It's incredible how certain kids are great when you are one-on-one with them, but a certain chemistry takes place when the whole group gets together, and everything goes up for grabs. Get to know the individuals who make up your group instead of treating the entire youth group as a single entity.

Be a Good Listener

We youth leaders expect young people to listen to us, but all too frequently we don't take the time to listen to them. When a person who is important to us does not listen to our concerns, we begin to feel we must not be worth much. This can be especially true for young people, whose lives are a series of confusing changes. Kids need to know their adult youth leaders will listen to those things that are important to them. The adult youth leader who won't listen, or who responds to a student's concerns with statements like "We can't take the time now to talk about that," or "That's off the subject," is probably making the student feel put down or put off.

Real listening does not necessarily mean agreement. It does mean making the effort to clarify and understand another person's feelings and point of view.

Real listening requires that we attend to more than just the spoken words, since nonverbal messages often carry more weight than words. Look at the posture of the other person as she speaks, and watch her gestures. Try to hear the feelings or the mood behind her words. And your body language should communicate care and acceptance back to the speaker, rather than judgment or disinterest. Remember that your body language acts out what you are feeling, and avoid the following body language that is inappropriate for a listener:

- Turning your back to the person speaking
- Folding arms and leaning back as the person is speaking
- Drumming your finger on a table or chair
- Not maintaining eye contact
- Yawning
- Distancing yourself from the person speaking
- Frowning or having a scolding look as the person speaks
- Rummaging through a drawer or cupboard—or otherwise moving around while a person speaks
- Checking your wristwatch or a clock

As the listener, you must be accepting of the individual. This does not necessarily mean you agree with everything that's said, or that you accept the situation the person is in—only that you accept the person. As the listener, you must take the time and the interest to listen, and communicate that nonverbally:

- Lean forward toward the student.
- Smile when appropriate. It expresses love and acceptance.
- Maintain eye contact.
- Move close to the student without violating his or her space.
- Nod your head as the student is speaking.
- Ask open-ended questions.
- Don't be satisfied with the first response: Reflect, summarize, compare and contrast, probe.

Adult youth leaders must help students feel free to express their thoughts and feelings. Set limits on behavior, not on opinions. A healthy youth group provides a space where opinions can be freely expressed (as long as proper rules of courtesy are maintained). Working toward this goal will help create an atmosphere in which people feel accepted and learn to listen to one another.

Forgive and Forget

Dredging up past mistakes for review is bad business—period. Once a situation has been dealt with and discipline has been dished out, forget it. A student's current situation and behavior, what's happening or not happening, can be criticized, but your message should only concern what's going on at that time. Don't take a particular incident as an opportunity to throw everything but the kitchen sink into your message.

Since neither you nor your kids have perfect judgment, it's best to err on the side of being too forgiving, rather than not forgiving enough. Author Warren W. Wiersbe learned this lesson in parenting his own kids:

> If I err, I want to err on the side of forgiveness. There were probably times when I should have walloped the kids. Only now I am finding out things they did I never knew before—by listening to my son preach! He'll tell a story from his teens and I'll say, "I didn't know about that." But they seemed to have come through.
>
> On the other hand there were times when we disciplined the kids for things they didn't do. I discovered the truth later. Fortunately, where there's love, openness, honesty, and fun, kids somehow survive those injustices.
>
> Oh—a sense of humor really helps!

Isolating a Student

When a young person seems unable to control his behavior, separating that student from the group can be an effective consequence. A short period of isolation is a safe and effective way of handling an individual who is emotionally upset. It gives a breather to that student, the leader, and the entire group. It often removes the young person from the cause of his trouble. He can be asked to step outside the room to speak with another adult leader in the ministry or just to wait with an adult volunteer until you are free to talk with him or to set up a meeting at some future time.

One positive effect of sending a young person outside the room for misbehavior is that it communicates that not being involved in a group activity is a punishment; therefore, the youth room must be a great place to be. So more students behave so they can participate.

One drawback to isolating a particular student is that his perception may be, "The youth leaders don't know what to do with me, so they are getting rid of me." For this reason you'll want to make sure you don't overuse the technique with any particular student, and that you continue to communicate your desire to have this student as part of the group.

Another form of isolation is to separate two young people who are constantly fighting. Either have an adult sit between them or ask them not to sit together. The crazy thing is that most rowdy kids have a built-in magnet that attracts them to other rowdy kids. You can also ask your adult leaders to sit by kids who might be a challenge, without letting the students know why the adults are sitting nearby.

Follow Up

It's important to make the time to have a conversation with the young person who has caused a disturbance. If it's not possible to have such a talk at the time of the incident or immediately after it, make a point of following up within the next couple of days. When you discuss what happened, use the eye/name/touch/gesture method. Make eye contact with the person and make sure she is looking at you. Call her by name. Touch the student gently on the shoulder, and then gesture with your other hand as you describe the problem and why you separated her from the group. Share what you are trying to accomplish in the youth group and ask for her help. Let the offender know you are personally hurt.

Reflect grief through your facial expressions.

I find the **SODAS** acronym designed by Boys Town to be helpful when talking to the individual:

Situation: Have the student explain what happened in his own words, telling you the situation and what caused the misbehavior.

Options: Have the student suggest some other options that were available at the time. What were the alternatives to what he said or did? The student may start with silly ideas, but if you maintain a straight face, eventually he'll begin to share some practical ideas.

Disadvantages: Have him go through the options and share the disadvantages of each alternative action.

Advantages: Have him go through the list of options and talk about the advantages of each alternative action.

Solution/Simulation: Help the student decide on a more constructive solution for the next time this situation arises. You may want to do a little simulation or role-playing of the events that caused the misbehavior, to try out this alternative response.

I like the way the SODAS method shows students what they've done wrong. It helps students own their own actions and keeps their dignity intact as they work toward strategies for solving problems. Students are far more likely to follow strategies they've created than behavior that's been assigned to them.

Complete your conversation with a brief time of prayer. Pray that you hope the things discussed today will meet the student's needs at the next meeting. Your prayer helps to emphasize that you see this student as a valuable asset to the youth group.

If you decide the best way to talk over a problem with a student is by meeting them for lunch, be sure you don't frame that as a punishment. Don't make it sound like having to spend time with you is a terrible thing.

Too often problem kids hear from adults only when they're in trouble; our rowdies need extra attention, especially when they are not misbehaving.

Compensate for any disciplinary action with positive attention.

Even if you have an opportunity to discuss the event immediately after it occurred, you should be sure to make some kind of contact with the person you've disciplined within a few days of the incident. Don't let distance grow between you and troublemakers. A good policy is to follow up with every person you've disciplined within two days.

Ignoring

Sometimes the best way to encourage students to behave in a more mature and responsible manner is to ignore certain kinds of misbehavior, rather than drawing attention to them. When ignoring is selected as a consequence to misbehavior, the young person is being told that some behaviors are so childish, they are not worthy of a response. If you've told a student certain behavior is annoying and unacceptable, and he or she continues that behavior, sometimes the best thing to do is ignore the young person. Instead of giving attention, take away the reinforcement. Be sure students don't get the wrong idea—that you are condoning misbehavior by ignoring it.

When the misbehaving young person behaves acceptably, interact with him. Demonstrate that you will ignore him only when he acts

"O son, son...where did your youth pastor go wrong?"

immaturely. As soon as the young person behaves as expected, he is a contributing member of the youth group.

Eliminate or Reduce Sweet Treats

Youth leaders have long observed that some kids go bonkers after eating foods with a lot of artificial sweeteners. Medical researchers—not to mention the food industry—have been more skeptical. But a carefully designed study published in 2007 in the British medical journal *The Lancet* shows that a variety of common food dyes and the preservative sodium benzoate–an ingredient in many soft drinks, fruit juices, and salad dressings–do cause some kids to become measurably more hyperactive and distractible. The findings prompted Britain's Food Standards Agency to issue an immediate advisory to parents to limit their children's intake of additives if they notice an effect on behavior. At this point there hasn't been a similar response in the United States, but doctors say it makes sense for parents and youth leaders to be on the alert.

The paper in *The Lancet* may be the first to prove a link between additives and hyperactivity, but back in the 1970s this idea was the basis for the restrictive Feingold diet, which was popularized as a treatment for AD/HD. Some clinicians still routinely advise parents of kids with AD/HD to steer their kids away from preservatives and food dyes. "It matters for some kids, so I tell parents to be their own scientist," says psychiatrist Edward Hallowell, author of several books on AD/HD. While a similar link between hyperactivity and sugar remains unproven, Hallowell cautions parents to watch sweets, too. "I've seen too many kids who flip out after soda and birthday cake," he says. "I urge them to eat whole foods. They'll be healthier anyway." (For more on ministering among AD/HD kids, see chapter 14.)

Youth groups can often lower the number of disruptive occurrences by limiting sweets at youth meetings. Many youth groups are also offering high-nutrition foods with low levels of stimulants. Some youth groups are replacing candy and other sweet snacks with fruit.

Teasing

If one of your students is having difficulty with being teased by other young people, emphasize to that student you cannot make the other kids stop teasing by punishing them. Make it clear that the youth leaders understand her frustrations, but let her know that the most effective way to stop the teasing will be to change her own reactions. The easiest and most effective way to eliminate chronic teasing is for the victim to completely ignore it. Explain that immature young people will tease her to see her reaction; that's the whole point of teasing. Point out that when she reacts to teasing, she is rewarding her tormentors.

Have the young person make a list of the kinds of words, names, and comments that have bothered her. Go through the list, beginning with the names and comments that bother her least, and help her see how she can respond. You might even try some role-playing—but do this only if the young person wants to participate.

Young people find it much easier to ignore teasing or to laugh it off when they have good self-images. By working to build a young person's self-confidence, you can help her feel strong enough to ignore teasing.

Using Excuses

Some kids (and some adults) seem to have an excuse for everything:

- Striking out at baseball ("The sun was in my eyes.")
- Getting in trouble at school ("It was the teacher's fault.")
- Failing to turn in the deposit for the youth retreat on time ("I thought it was due next week.")
- Using putdowns ("She started it!")
- Not turning off a cell phone ("I'm expecting an important call.")
- Always being late ("There was a traffic jam." "The dog ate my alarm clock." "An evil monkey hid my pants." "There was a rip in the space-time continuum.")

One of my favorite excuses ever was one I heard on Court TV. A teenager was pulled over by the police for driving a car 93 miles per hour. His excuse? "I had to get home to catch the school bus."

A young person who always offers excuses feels she can avoid being accountable for her own behavior. In the past her excuses probably helped her get out of work and avoid negative consequences for her actions. Since the strategy has been effective, making excuses has become a habit. Even though the habit may have begun innocently, young people need to understand that such behavior makes them unreliable.

Other young people who make up excuses may also be in need of attention. They've learned that making excuses can be a way to manipulate adults and receive a lot of immediate and individualized attention.

Your response should vary depending on the young person. A mild verbal reprimand can be used with young people who are unaware of their behavior and are likely to improve once they realize their responses are inappropriate. If a young person seems to need attention, ignoring the excuses is the most effective strategy to respond. The student must learn that giving excuses will not earn your attention. Find a time when you can discuss the problem with the young person and explain that you want to trust her, but you are having difficulty knowing when to believe what she says.

HE SAID NUTHIN' ABOUT CASTING SPITWADS.

If junior highers had been in the crowd

© 1994 Dik LaPine

Swearing

Until 10 years ago the diagnostic manual of the American Psychiatry Association (APA) listed adolescent cursing as a symptom of something called "oppositional defiance disorder." But the APA dropped cursing from its manual in 1998 because "normal" kids were swearing as much as "problem" kids.

Many young people swear because such language is part of their environment. If they have parents or peers who swear, and if they hear such language frequently in movies and music, it can become a natural part of their speech—a habit, much like saying "you know." They may not even be aware their language is offensive to others.

Many teens feel swearing is no big deal. (A recent survey determined that about 60 percent of teens feel swearing is morally acceptable, while only 20 percent of people in their 60s and 70s accept this.) Some young people believe such language allows them to express themselves more powerfully. Other young people think it makes them appear more sophisticated, more mature, or tough. Still others swear to antagonize adults and get attention. Four-letter words often express a teen's inability to say what he means—and that may be because he doesn't really know how. The F-word gets used because it can mean anything and nothing and everything all at once.

While there are more serious challenges facing teens than the occasional four-letter word, this subject still needs to be addressed by those who work with teenagers. In November of 2007, the principal of St. Clare of Montefalco Catholic School near Detroit had students stay after a Mass and informed the fifth through eighth graders cursing was unacceptable at the school. Just in case anyone was uncertain about what words she meant, Sister Kathy Avery read off a list of the very words and phrases she was banning. "It got a little quiet in church" during her talk, she told the *Detroit Free Press*. Some parents were shocked, but the newspaper quoted others who applauded Sister Kathy's effort:

> "In a way you would think a nun would shy away from something like that, but she's very open with the children, very clear in her messages," said Margaret Roache, chairperson of the school commission. Roache's sixth-grade son was there when Avery read the list of banned words. "When I asked him to give me a sample of it, he said, 'Oh, no, I can't say it!'" Roache said. "I thought it was great."

Incidentally, curse words aren't the only things that set Avery off. She's also banned the words *stupid* and *boring*.

If the language of your group is a problem, choose a neutral time to explain to your youth group that you are concerned about the amount of swearing you hear. Explain that swearing is inappropriate and offensive to many people. Warn them that some people will judge them solely on the basis of their language. Let students know that offensive language is prohibited in your youth group. You may want to make it part of your youth group's code of conduct. Encourage students to become more articulate in expressing their feelings, thoughts, and views and do so as clearly as possible. If the problem persists, talk to individual students who are involved. Explain the consequences if the swearing continues.

Racial and ethnic slurs are among the most destructive vulgar language, and I'd encourage every youth pastor to take a very firm stance against these. The NAACP held a ceremonial burying of the N-word in New York City on July 9, 2007. The group recognizes this will not necessarily stop the use of racially offensive language, but their action helps make the world aware of the concern over this kind of language and the ways in which offensive language can often escalate into aggressive behavior. I believe we need a zero-tolerance policy for such language within our ministries. We need to maintain an atmosphere of respect in our youth groups.

In their book *Teens In Turmoil*, Carol Maxym and Leslie B. York point out two other "four-letter words" teens tend to use that they find distressing—*like* and *just*.

These two words are the great minimizers. Teens use "just" when they want you to think whatever they did isn't so bad, and "like" when they want to mean that nothing is ever really anything. Suddenly there is almost no meaning in the communication. While these two words may seem innocuous, pay attention when your teen's use of them is primarily to manipulate or minimize.

Four Discipline Don'ts

I've spent most of this chapter offering a variety of ideas about what you can do to respond effectively to everyday discipline challenges. But before we close, let's look at a few important "don'ts" of discipline:

Don't expect you'll always be popular.

When youth leaders complain they can't control their young people, I frequently ask, "Do they do what you ask them to do?" The answer is often, "Yeah, they do it—but I don't like the way they do it. It's their attitude, you see." When I pursue the issue, I find that many leaders think teens should not only be compliant, but also should be delighted over the opportunity to comply.

But teenagers are usually not happy about being corrected—that's a lesson we all learn eventually. One ministry I worked with had a rule that no smoking was allowed during our week at camp. One year, a counselor saw a kid lighting up during free time. Since this kid had never camped with us before, the counselor went to the young person, explained the rule, and asked the camper to put out the cigarette. The camper complied, but the counselor was upset the student didn't look thrilled at being told he wouldn't be allowed to smoke all week. Rather than getting bent out of shape, the counselor probably should have been appreciative that the camper complied with his wishes. Agreeing not to smoke for the week may have been very difficult for this kid—especially since he didn't share the counselor's opinion on the value of cigarette smoking (or lack of it).

Don't expect your students will like every single thing you ask them to do. Simply because you want a young person to stop a certain behavior does not mean she'll no longer have that desire. Don't hassle a kid who complies just because she doesn't seem happy about it. I'm not saying you should accept backtalk or nastiness, but don't declare war just because the kid has an expression on her face that says, "This is a dumb rule." Don't even try to convince her immediately that it is a good rule. You can explain your reasoning at a later time when the person is ready to talk.

Don't embarrass teenagers publicly.

If you've spent hours preparing a lesson, the last thing you want is a disruption in the group. It can be tempting to say something in response that might embarrass the troublemaker, and make him or her feel humiliated. But before you do so, consider the consequences.

Teenagers are incredibly self-conscious. Your remark may stop the troublemaking behavior, but the resulting embarrassment could cost you a group member. And that one embarrassed teenager will probably tell five or six friends what you did—and you may lose them, too. Most outbursts are designed to get your attention. You reward troublemakers when you stop everything to focus on them.

Don't resort to destructive criticism or name-calling.

A pinch of constructive criticism is part of the recipe for any good youth group. Unfortunately, many youth leaders shovel the criticism out by the truckload—and that can do more harm than good.

Here are some helpful hints on using criticism constructively. First of all, critique the behavior, not the person. Criticizing someone lowers that person's self-esteem and feelings of self-worth. Separate the behavior from the person.

Remember that it takes eight positive comments to make up for a single negative one—and that includes those critical comments we intend to be constructive. Be sensitive to the individual. Share your insights with a young person at a time when he's not surrounded by his peers, when both of you are not rushed, and after you've taken time to gain his respect.

Maybe a young person has a problem with hygiene and you know other kids are avoiding him because of his body odor. This problem needs to be pointed out to the young person, but it must be done very gently—not with a condemning attitude, but with a spirit of love and support. If you are going to point out a problem or concern, make sure you also offer practical solutions; otherwise your criticism can merely destroy the person you want to help.

No matter what happens, never resort to name-calling. All teenagers have certain imperfections about which they are overly sensitive. The world takes notice of them to tease and ridicule. If a teenager is small, he's called "shorty," "squirt," "shrimp," or "runt." If he's tall and thin, he's "beanpole" or "stick." If he's overweight, it might be "fatso" or "blimp." If he's weak or uncoordinated, he might be "wimp" or "geek." Teenagers suffer deeply from such nicknames, even when they feign indifference.

In general it's best for adult leaders to avoid teasing their young people, even in jest. Insults cut deeper and last longer when they come from an adult youth leader. We can learn to communicate without sarcasm and ridicule. There is no place for biting comments in conversations between adult leaders and young people. Sarcasm evokes hatred and provokes counterattacks.

Criticism of personality and character gives a young person negative feelings about herself. A young person who is made to feel stupid accepts such evaluation as fact. She may give up intellectual pursuits to escape ridicule. Since competition means failure, her safety depends on not trying.

Don't threaten what you cannot or will not do.

Have you ever gotten so frustrated—after trying every method imaginable to quiet your group—that you yelled out a threat so idiotic your kids knew you would never follow through on it? Something similar to, "If you kids don't shut up, I'll never allow you to go on another church activity as long as you live!" They may stop the noise for a second, until they realize you'd never do such a thing. Empty threats don't help at all. In fact, such false statements just let kids know they have you!

The freshmen who enter our youth group each September are often a bit intimidated because they are the youngest ones in the group. One skit we do each year breaks the ice and helps those young people get a glimpse of one aspect of our discipline methods. As the young people come into the room on a particular week, I start trying to quiet them down—but I don't try very hard. Eventually, I pretend I'm getting mad and finally yell out, "If you kids don't shut up, I'm going to rip your arms off!"

Well, it always gets deadly silent—except for one eleventh-grader in the front row who continues to talk loudly. I walk directly to that student (who's still talking) and repeat, "I told you—if you don't shut up, I'm going to rip your arms off." At this point you could hear a pin drop in the room. Every eye is on me and this one young person (who is still the only one talking). I reach over and grab him by the arm...

What the new freshmen don't know is that I got together with this eleventh-grader before the meeting and fixed him up so he has a mannequin's arm up his sleeve. After I grab the arm, I yank it right out of his sleeve. The freshmen kids in the back are screaming, "He did it! He really did it!" The kids quickly realize we were kidding—and everybody has a good laugh. But then I explain that if we say we're going to do something in this youth group, they can bet we will follow through on it.

Now Ask Yourself

1. Think of a situation in which you could have been a better listener. What went wrong?

2. Do you struggle with the desire to be popular with your kids? How does this hinder your discipline with them?

3. Have you ever employed criticism or name-calling? What was the result?

4. What do you communicate to young people nonverbally?

5. Do you set limits on behavior and not on opinions? Do your young people feel comfortable talking to you about anything? How can you make yourself more accessible and create an atmosphere where questions and opinions are encouraged?

6. Are you a forgiving person? Remember Jesus' story of the unmerciful servant who was forgiven a huge debt he owed, but would not forgive the guy who owed him a few dollars (Matthew 18:21-35)? Who are you in the story?

Coping with Caustic Kids

Like most other youth ministers, I've been burned time and again by a certain kind of kid. These kids are difficult to love. They've got a calloused outer shell that's difficult to penetrate. They don't laugh or cry. They seem to have cut themselves off from all emotion. It's hard to read what they are feeling at any specific moment. They've created a protective barrier around themselves, often because of emotional pain from past experiences.

I call such hardened young people "caustic kids." The word *caustic* comes from the same root as the word *cauterize*, a medical term that means to burn until a wound is closed off. Caustic kids are kids who have burned relationships with peers and those in authority over them to the point where almost all their relationships have been closed off.

Caustic kids are tremendously difficult to work with. The tendency is to want to pull in the welcome mat. These are hardened kids. Nothing you say or do seems to connect with them. They may be in trouble with the law.

What I have discovered over the years, however, is that many of these kids are like Tootsie Pops. You know, that little round candy on the end of a stick. They are very hard on the outside, but once you get past that outer shell there is something soft and good in the center. Caustic kids are like that. Once you get past the calloused, hard veneer that covers them, there is a wonderful kid on the inside—a kid that just needs to be loved.

Why Caustic Kids Are Tough to Work With

If you're one who shies away from kids like this, I don't blame you. They're hard to love. It's natural to distance yourself from them. They give you lots of reasons not to like them:

1. Caustic kids tend to be self-centered. They don't have winsome personalities. Often they're not even pleasant. These kids share a "gift" for pushing people away.

2. They don't respect you or your position. They defy you at every step. Caustic kids refuse to cooperate. They interrupt you with snide remarks. They undermine your authority by breaking rules. They try their best to lag behind and not participate. Caustic kids call the youth programs boring, and they're not shy about criticizing you around other students.

3. Caustic kids can sabotage your ministry. These kids are happy to talk bad about you to anyone who will listen—including their parents and other kids in the group. Caustic kids can jeopardize your relationships with parents, other youth leaders, other teenagers, your senior pastor, and the church board.

4. They're a threat to your "success ratio." Your inability to break through caustic kids' rough exteriors can lead others to think you don't know how to handle difficult cases. They're a nagging reminder you may not be as outstanding as you'd hoped.

5. They're a living illustration of what you're trying to keep your kids from becoming. Caustic kids love to look and act like they're from "the wrong crowd." They tell magnetic stories about the parties they've gone to, movies they've seen, the classes they've skipped, the people they have cut, the guns they own, and the joyrides they've taken in stolen cars.

6. They're an ever-present irritant. Caustic kids bring the worst kind of music along on the church bus. They tune out everyone as they retreat beneath headphones. They sneak off to smoke cigarettes…or worse.

7. They are probably a lot like you! Most youth leaders are strong-willed—just like these kids. You run into conflicts with these kids because like forces repel each other. Sparks fly!

At one time nitric acid was used to determine whether a certain ore was real gold or fool's gold. If the mineral passed "the acid test," it was gold. The same is true for caustic kids. Their "acidic" behavior is a true test of the purity of your ministry and your commitment to loving kids—even those who seem least lovable.

The junior high boys Bible study finally pushed Youth Pastor Craig too far.

"Hey guys, meet you're new study leader, Joe Luzinski. He felt a call to volunteer with the group after 20 years as a Marine drill sergeant. And let me tell ya, he's a real cut-up, so just be yourselves around him!"

© 1997 Andrew Toos

Why We Need to Work with Caustic Kids

Though caustic kids offer us plenty of reasons to pull in the welcome mat, there are compelling reasons we must minister to them:

1. Jesus commands us to love the unlovable. Jesus says, "If you love those who love you, what reward will you get? Are not even the tax collectors doing that?" (Matthew 5:46). The true test of love is loving people who don't love back.

2. Few adults have the maturity and perspective to love unlikable kids. Those who have this ability are rare and precious. They can literally turn a young person's life around.

3. Your ministry is the last hope for many caustic kids. If the church rejects troublemakers, the only group left for them to join is "the wrong crowd." This is the truth: Whoever values your kids most, and shows it, usually wins them over.

   Eugene Rivers is an inner-city pastor hoping to rescue a Boston neighborhood from drugs and poverty. He tells the story of a conversation he had with a heroin dealer. The heroin dealer told Rivers his key to success was simply being there. Rivers asked, "Being there?" The drug dealer went on to explain, "When little Johnny goes to school—I am there. When little Johnny goes to the store for food, I'm there. I'm there—and you're not. I'm there, so I win."

4. Deviant kids look for ways to justify their antisocial behavior. If you reject these kids, they'll use your rejection to justify their wrongdoing.

5. Caustic kids are hypersensitive about being treated unfairly. Troubled kids often judge an adult's worth by how fair he or she seems to be. That's why it's imperative that you respond to your troublemakers fairly. It may not be fair for them to treat you poorly and expect to always be treated fairly by you, but they will, nevertheless.

6. Troublemakers aren't as tough as they seem. Caustic kids are ripe for ministry when they get into trouble. Many are genuinely afraid of what might happen to them. Don't bruise the fruit the way one Houston minister did. He got permission to visit a teenager at a drug-treatment center. The first thing he said was: "I'm here to ask you one question. Are you the one who stole the hubcaps off my car?" Blunders like this one explain why many health-care workers cast a suspicious eye toward people in pastoral ministry.

7. You may know what certain kids do, but you may not know the "why." Beneath the hard exterior of most caustic kids is often enormous pain and frustration. When you minister to these kids instead of rejecting them, you give them the benefit of the doubt.

8. Caustic kids tend to be very strong-willed, and strong-willed kids are tomorrow's leaders. Compliant kids may be easier to minister to, but they may not accomplish nearly as much with

what you teach them. Reach a strong-willed teenager and he or she will often multiply your ministry many times over. History shows that countless strong-willed kids who were channeled in the right direction grew up to save nations from tyranny and people from hopelessness.

9. Ministry to tough kids keeps you from going soft. Kids who love you, hug you, and hang on your every word make ministry fun. But tough kids make ministry challenging. They keep you digging, praying, reading books, and sharing with other youth leaders. Above all, they keep you growing.

10. Jesus said he came "to seek and to save what was lost" (Luke 19:10). Caustic kids are as lost as can be—and as Jesus' followers, we need to follow him in seeking them out. "Seek" is the key word here. Caustic kids need you to take the initiative. They don't realize they are lost. They think they're okay when they're really self-destructing.

Caustic kids are often arrogantly self-destructive, blindly ego-centered, dangerously unconcerned about their rejection of Christianity, and rude toward anyone who tries to reach out to them. In short, these kids are proud of the things they should feel ashamed of. They need your help.

Jesus once asked the scribes and Pharisees, "Suppose one of you has a hundred sheep and loses one of them. Doesn't he leave the ninety-nine in the open country and go after the lost sheep until he finds it?" (Luke 15:4). I love Buddy Scott's paraphrase of Jesus' answer: "I say to you that likewise, there will be more joy in heaven over one caustic kid who repents than over 99 model kids who need no repentance"(v. 7).

Ministering to Caustic Kids

We have an obligation to reach out to strong-willed kids. But what do you do with lost kids who are so disruptive and difficult they seem to be threatening your entire ministry?

If your youth group has ever been damaged by such kids, you might not be surprised to learn that the word *caustic* has the same root as the word *holocaust*. Caustic kids have the power to ruin your entire ministry. You're compelled to minister to them, but you're not compelled to let them destroy your ministry. But it can be a fine line.

If lost young people pose a serious threat in the group setting, you may need to pull them out of that environment and minister to them individually. But this needs to be done with great care. Take such measures only after meeting with parents and other pastoral staff to develop a "united front" for rescuing kids while protecting the youth group.

"My parents gave me $5 to come. For $7.50, I'll go back home."

Caustic youth require a long-term commitment. Conditions will probably get worse before they get better. To be effective, the relationship must be long term. Caustic kids will require you to change your expectations about how kids will respond to you. Here are some expectations that must change:

- Caustic kids will appreciate you.
- Caustic kids will trust you.
- Caustic kids will obey you.
- Caustic kids will be honest with you.

- Caustic kids will be open to the gospel.
- Caustic kids will want to change.
- Caustic kids will accept your values.
- Caustic kids will accept your advice.
- Caustic kids will become responsible.
- Caustic kids will want to be loved.

Building relationships and communicating with caustic kids is not easy, but we really shouldn't expect it to be. In 1 Corinthians 13:7, the apostle Paul reminds us that genuine love "always protects, always trusts, always hopes, always perseveres." This kind of love involves paying the price and having realistic expectations and commitment. It will be tough, but God calls us to nothing less than selfless love over the long haul. And he will change lives through you.

Brick-Wall Youth Groups

Dealing with just one or two caustic kids can be plenty difficult. But sometimes you'll run into a situation where the entire youth group is made up of caustic kids. I call this a "brick-wall youth group"—because trying to get these kids to do anything feels a lot like talking to a brick wall (or maybe banging your head against one!)

The kids in a brick-wall group are stubborn, ornery, and rude. The spirit of the entire group is negative, cynical, and sarcastic. No matter what you do or say, kids will mock and challenge you. A brick-wall group seems to take pride in the number of youth leaders it can force into early retirement. And one of the most frightening things about a brick-wall group is that it scares "good" youth group members away.

Discipline doesn't always work in a brick-wall group. Trust me—I've tried. I talked to the whole group. I spoke with kids individually. I held retreats on spiritual "lukewarmness." The senior minister even talked with the group. But none of my usual approaches seemed to work with this group.

Fortunately, quitting isn't the only way to deal with a brick-wall group. But it's essential to take a future-oriented approach. Don't expect a sudden turnaround. Change won't happen overnight. In fact, you should expect it to be painful for the first 12 to 18 months.

One of the most effective approaches with such a group is to pull out the key "bricks." Even though your group may have a number of troublesome kids, it's likely that there are a few key bricks. If you can remove those primary troublemakers, the wall will fall down.

One way to determine which kids are the key bricks is to ask yourself: "If the youth group gets noisy, who could tell the group to quiet down and the group would listen?" These are your key kids. They are your leaders—even if they don't lead the group in the direction you'd like.

Now when I say "pull out," I don't mean kick these kids out of the group—at least not immediately. I mean pull these kids aside and find out their chief concerns. I invited a few key bricks out for pizza one night. I asked them to tell me what they thought of the youth group. Most were surprisingly candid. They told me what they liked and disliked. I also learned that many of them were carrying around a lot of hurt inside. Some felt rejected by the church or pushed into Christianity by their parents. After the pizza outing, these kids seemed more open. And when the key kids change their attitude, it has a dramatic effect on the entire group.

You'll also need the support of other adults to work successfully with a brick-wall group. Such kids can cause you to lose your self-confidence. When your efforts are continually frustrated, you begin to think you're a failure. You need people around you to show you you're not crazy. You can minister to kids. Find volunteers to help you.

Finally, and most importantly, it's essential to pray. In Mark 9:14-29 the disciples run into a situation that seems impossible. But in verse 29, Jesus reminds them there is something they can do: "This kind can come out only by prayer."

The hurt and hardness of caustic kids can be softened only by the tenderness of God's Holy Spirit. And that comes by prayer. Don't spend your prayer time asking that the activities in your group would go well. Instead, pray that the kids in your group would experience the love and healing power of God.

Though he'd left the church more than an hour ago, youth worker Sammy Jenkins couldn't shake the feeling that Junior High Night was not quite over yet.

© 1990 Dan Pegoda

Now Ask Yourself

1. Describe some characteristics of a caustic kid you've worked with. How did you work with him?

2. If you could start over again, what changes would you make in your approach to this student?

3. Which of the 10 reasons for ministering to caustic kids resonated most with you and why?

4. What steps could you take to be more effective in working with brick-wall youth groups?

12

Antidotes to Apathy

Another area that drives many youth leaders up the wall is the "I don't care" attitude that affects so many youth groups.

Today's young people are not apathetic out of ignorance. Due to technologies that deliver news from every corner of our shrinking globe to our TV and computer screens, kids are more aware than ever before that they live in a world of great need. And many of today's kids care deeply about the world, their families, their youth groups, and vital issues of life and death, right and wrong.

But more than youth of former generations, today's kids often feel powerless to make a difference. When television delivers graphic stories of bloody conflicts or starving children, when newspaper headlines shout about gang wars and random violence, when the pastor preaches the plight of unsaved millions, today's teenagers often ask, "What could I possibly do about all this?" Young people suffer from an identity crisis, a feeling of smallness in the midst of overwhelming challenges. And that feeling of powerlessness quickly leads to apathy.

The teenagers of previous generations dealt with issues that hit close to home. During their own teenage years, the parents and grandparents of today's kids often had to work to help support the family or care for younger siblings and older relatives. Their contributions were concrete. But today's issues are often systemic, global, and catastrophic. As a result, teenagers feel powerless, and many of them feel the only way they can cope is to withdraw. Though these kids are criticized for being apathetic and selfish, this behavior isn't the result of self-preoccupation, but rather a deep struggle with questions of their own competence and significance.

The situation has been echoed in the church. In the past young people felt more like they were part of the larger church body. There weren't nearly as many programs and ministries devoted specifically to their age group. Kids found ways to involve themselves in the church's ministry. I often wonder if our well-intentioned attempts to create programs of interest to teens have unwittingly contributed to teenagers' feelings of apathy. Often ministry is done to or for them instead of with them. When "adults" run all the programs, young people are left on the sidelines—relegated to their own group of peers. This also contributes to the feeling of helplessness that leads to apathy.

Inspire Them to Greatness

Our role as adult youth leaders is clear. We must inspire young people to greatness, by helping young people see themselves as God's agents of change in this world. We overcome apathy by providing our students with a sense of calling that generates unparalleled enthusiasm for life.

We youth ministers have mistakenly assumed the best way to reach young people is to provide them with various forms of entertainment. Maybe instead we should be much more focused on inviting young people to accept the challenge to become heroes and change the world. By helping students believe God has called them to participate in the remaking of society, we can inspire them to action and deliver them from the deadness of the spirit we call *apathy*.

Sixteen-year-old Zach Hunter has found a way to make a difference in the lives of people who are hurting. For the past four years, Zach has been working to end slavery around the globe. Although many people (maybe even you) think slavery was eliminated long ago, the sad truth is that there are more people bound in slavery now than at any other time in history. Zach founded an organization called Loose Change to Loosen Chains (www.lc2lc.org) that's mobilizing students to help end slavery and free the men, women, and children who are being held against their will. He's also written a book called *Be the Change* (Zondervan, 2007), in which he talks about his own efforts to end slavery and encourages other young people to find the area of their own passion—and then go out and do something heroic for God.

Savannah Rose Walters is a 14-year-old Florida student who's encouraging people to pump up their tires to save the Arctic Refuge. This hero began her ministry in the second grade when she was studying the Arctic and its animals. She wanted to protect the environment, and she realized that getting people to properly inflate their car tires could have a huge impact. The U.S. Department of Energy has stated, "In 2005 Americans wasted 1.2 billion gallons of gas by driving on underinflated tires." Eighty-five percent of American cars are driven with too little air in their tires—which leads to poor fuel efficiency and the increased depletion of natural resources. By educating drivers about the importance of inflating their tires, Savannah is not only working to preserve the environment by reducing air pollution and cutting down on the need for domestic oil drilling; she's also helping people save money. Savannah's initiative has inspired Pump 'em Up events across 15 states and has distributed more than 10,000 tire gauges to the newly educated drivers. She has also spoken alongside U.S. senators in Washington, DC. She is a hero. Check out her Web site at www.pumpemup.org.

As a middle school student, Ryan Hreljac saved his allowance and worked odd jobs to get enough money to buy a well in Africa. What motivated him to do this? Someone told him that one out of every six people on the earth does not have access to safe drinking water. According to UNICEF lack of safe water and sanitation is the world's single largest cause of illness. Ryan got other students to participate in building wells and eventually started the Ryan's Well Foundation, which has now built more than 300 wells in 14 countries, bringing clean water to nearly half a million people. Ryan is a hero. (For more info, visit www.ryanswell.ca.)

Connecting Biblical Truths and Teenage Realities

Another reason many church kids seem apathetic is because they feel churches are out of touch. Our churches often do a poor job of connecting biblical truths to teenage realities. We have to rethink ministry to this group. And that begins by focusing on meeting senior highers' real needs. And many youth ministries just aren't doing that.

According to a Search Institute study, "Effective Christian Education: A National Study of Protestant Congregations," one out of three church-going teenagers has had sexual intercourse by the eleventh or twelfth grade. Yet only 27 percent of Christian teenagers say their churches emphasize sex education.

Forty-two percent of churchgoing eleventh- and twelfth-graders admit to drinking alcohol six or more times within the past year, yet only 20 percent of kids say the church stresses drug and alcohol education.

Typically, youth ministers have strong opinions about what kids need. But how many know what kids want to talk about? You may be surprised by the issues high schoolers hunger to learn more about.

Helping Teens Develop Close Relationships

We may also sense apathy from our students when they feel they have no close friends within the church. While senior highers often say their number one interest is learning to make new friends, only 38 percent of churchgoing teenagers feel their peers at church care about them. That means if you have 20 high schoolers in your youth group, it's likely that 12 of them feel unsupported by other group members. It can be very difficult to pinpoint which kids are feeling this way, since many of them look like they "fit in."

Close relationships are important in keeping both kids and adults involved in the church. Speaking at a meeting of the Religious Research Association, scholar Daniel Olson said if people have strong friendships within the church, they tend to continue attending, even if they become dissatisfied with various aspects of church life. For teenagers, both peer relationships and relationships with adults are crucial. "Churches can offer adolescents something available almost nowhere else in our culture: The interest, support, and care of adults," writes researcher Dorothy Williams in the Search Institute's newsletter, *Source*. "Nowhere else are there as many opportunities for interaction between people of widely different ages."

Transitioning from Youth to Adult

Churches can drive away senior highers with the very programming intended to keep young people involved. Many churches implement a rigorous education program for young people that goes until kids reach a certain age. When the training is finished, most churches accept the kids as full-fledged members. In theory, this practice is supposed to increase kids' commitment to the church. But in reality, it often gives kids the message that once they've finished the training, they've "graduated" from church. This "graduation mentality" is particularly true within churches that have a structured confirmation program to prepare young people to join the church. After completing confirmation, you often start seeing these kids only twice a year, at Christmas and Easter.

Search Institute researchers also found this trend in their study. "Two denominations (the Evangelical Lutheran Church in America and the United Church of Christ) with strong emphasis on thorough study in preparation for confirmation retain their levels of participation of youth in grades seven through nine," reports the Search Institute study. "However, for both of those denominations, percentages of participation for youth in grades ten through twelve…drop well below the participation rates of all other denominations."

To address this problem, some churches are holding their membership ceremonies for senior highers in the fall instead of the spring. That way, completion of confirmation or other membership training doesn't overlap with high school graduation. It's harder this way for kids to link confirmation to "being on my own." Other churches emphasize a long-term Christian education group, offering programs for older teenagers and adults that are just as exciting and challenging as the ones for younger kids.

Let Teens Spice Up Your Church

We've all heard teenagers say it: "Church is boring." In fact, this sense among kids that there's never anything exciting going on at church may be the primary reason many church kids seem apathetic. According to a study by the Search Institute, only 31 percent of churchgoing teenagers say church is interesting.

Although it's true that some youth will leave the church no matter what we do to make it more exciting or lively, we can't get caught up in blaming those who reject the church. Our task is to determine how we're part of the problem. I believe the sense that church is boring can be remedied relatively easily if a church is willing to make some changes.

One of those changes involves adopting a more experiential learning approach in your group programming. Get your senior highers moving, thinking, acting, laughing, crying, and relating with others, and you stand a good chance they'll want to stick around.

Boring programs invite misbehavior. I remember sitting in a large national gathering of adult youth ministers as a well-known writer spoke. Before he was through, half those youth workers had left because they were bored. The kids in our groups don't have the option of leaving if they get bored—so they simply look for other ways to entertain themselves.

Now I know the purpose of church isn't to entertain kids. But in this day of electronic games and devices, movies on demand, high-energy concerts, and the constant lure of the Internet—not to mention good-old omnipresent TV programming—we can't afford to be boring. At the same time, adult youth leaders need to explain to teens that most churches don't have a 16-station videogaming system, a 102-inch plasma screen HDTV, a skateboard park, and a bowling alley. Church will sometimes seem boring—but the same can be said for school, work, home, and life in general. If church bores your teens, help them find ways to spice it up. Encourage them to offer suggestions and volunteer their energy.

Did you ever hear a joke that doesn't seem funny—and then later you'll find yourself laughing about the punch line? We need to help kids see that church can be like that. Kids won't always come bouncing out of the church doors after worship on Sunday morning feeling spiritually revved up. In fact, there may be times when they leave wondering why they bothered going at all. But sooner or later something will click inside their heads. That sermon, Bible story, or worship experience will speak directly to them.

Delivering Students from a Highly Competitive World

Fear of failure can breed apathy in teenagers. When faced with the continual demands to achieve—whether it's grades, sports trophies, or popularity—many young people choose not to participate at all. Fearing failure, they find the easiest route is often simply to give up and declare they don't care.

Because students face so much pressure to compete in other areas of life, it's great to limit or eliminate competition within your youth group. Caring adult youth leaders will want to restructure their ministries and programs to provide an alternative to the stress of the highly competitive world in which teenagers live. Our churches should provide an environment in which acceptance doesn't have to be earned, in which young people will feel loved without having to prove themselves.

Set up programs and activities that don't encourage domination by superstars. Sports activities may seem like a healthy outlet for youth groups, but they are unhealthy when they simply become opportunities for the glorification of the already glorified or the degradation of the already put down. Sensitive adult youth leaders will encourage activities that neutralize the superior skills of some of the participants and that make having fun as a group the main purpose of recreation.

In *Growing Up in America*, Tony Campolo tells of a youth pastor who set up a volleyball game in which the net was 15 feet high. Her students played with a weather balloon instead of a volleyball, and the game was a crazy delight. Everyone participated as equals, and the fun came from cheering the movement of the balloon, which was more influenced by the wind than by their athletic prowess. The super jocks quickly learned they couldn't dominate, and the less athletic kids quickly gained confidence as full-fledged participants in the game. The game had everybody laughing, and winning was no big thing.

Embracing God's Grace

Apathy is part of our fallen condition as humans. In his book *The Road Less Traveled*, Harvard psychotherapist M. Scott Peck contends we are often too lazy and lethargic to make the life changes that will give us healthy dispositions and personal joy. Peck believes it is only by God's grace we can have the enthusiasm that dispels apathy. Isn't that what Paul said in Ephesians 2:4-5? "Because of his great love for us, God, who is rich in mercy, made us alive with Christ even when we were dead in transgressions—it is by grace you have been saved."

Our young people need spiritual regeneration to become young people who are wholly surrendered to what God wills to do in their lives. The Spirit gives life; without the Spirit people are dead, apathetic.

Søren Kierkegaard once claimed that the deadly sin of our age is the lack of passion. Passion for life is, ultimately, a gift from God. Let's challenge our young people and ourselves to rise from our apathetic morass and claim this most miraculous gift.

Now Ask Yourself

1. What are some of the worldwide events students are being exposed to on a weekly basis? How do you think this affects them?

2. What stories do you have of kids who reached out to other people?

3. How is your church making sure it is not out of touch with the real world of teens?

4. How do you foster community in your youth group? In this high-tech world how does your youth group encourage face-to-face interaction and deepened relationships?

5. If you have a confirmation class or something similar, what changes might you make to try to ensure that completion of the program does not result in "graduation" from church?

6. How have you been able to spice up your youth group time?

7. Is your youth group a safe place (emotionally, physically, and spiritually)?

8. How do you feel about Kierkegaard's statement that this generation lacks passion?

13

Helping High-Risk Kids

Randy is always quiet and withdrawn at youth gatherings. It's not just that he's an introvert. His is an aggressive silence—the kind that dares you to try to break through his tough exterior. Some of the kids in the group refer to him as "wasted" and "fried," and you've talked to his mother about Randy's history of drug and alcohol abuse. A year ago Randy went in for special treatment, and supposedly since then he has cleaned up his act. But you sometimes wonder if he's got everybody fooled and is really back into his old habits. Your efforts to get Randy involved always meet with resistance.

Sharon can be a real pain in group settings. She never takes anything seriously and spends most of her time giggling with her girlfriends or flirting with the guys in the group. You hear her talk a lot about the parties she attends, and you strongly suspect she's involved in sexual relationships. When you try to get her attention in Sunday school class or discipline her in private, she just rolls her eyes as if to say, "Whatever!"

Mike drives you up the wall. He drives the other kids up the wall, too, with his nonstop talking, practical jokes, and immature behavior. You know he's lacking a father figure since his parents' divorce, but your patience often runs out as he tests your limits time and again. Mike is more than merely active or rowdy. He has no regard for rules of any sort and has already had minor run-ins with the law for shoplifting, being caught with alcohol, and late-night drag racing. How can you discipline a kid like this?

Randy, Sharon, and Mike are all examples of high-risk young people. They are usually the kids who are in trouble—or are most likely to get into trouble. The paths they are on make their chances of future success low—the same problems you encounter with them at church pervade their home and school lives as well. These kids are primary candidates for depression, drug addiction, social isolation, teen pregnancy, and suicide. Many of them come from difficult family situations where parents are too busy struggling with their own problems to cope with their kids.

The one-on-one attention of a caring adult can really make a difference in the lives of high-risk young people. Kids like Randy, Sharon, and Mike need the support of a special person who takes the time to support and encourage small successes. The support person can keep in touch with a particular young person to see how he is doing, stay in contact with the parents, and work to disciple, motivate, and encourage the young person.

While counseling at junior-high camp, Steve hears that still, small voice calling him to a senior pastorate.

© 1991 Steve Phelps

Of course, you can't provide this amount of time to everyone. One alternative is to have a churchwide support team that pairs each high-risk student with a particular adult church member. But such a program needs to be established with the full recognition that you won't be able to help every young person. However, if 20 church members work with 20 high-risk young people, and half are successful, 10 young people will have learned they can be part of a system that cares. For a high-risk teen that might mean the difference between living productively in society or falling through the cracks.

Bullies

Bullying is seen among all age groups, even during the preschool years. It tends to increase through the elementary school years, and peaks during middle school and junior high, before declining only somewhat in high school. It's estimated that 7 percent to 13 percent of all schoolkids are bullies. About 10 percent of schoolkids are bullied but do not bully others, while about 6 percent both bully others and are bullied. In *Is My Teenager OK?* author Henry Paul says bullying includes behaviors such as hitting, extreme teasing, threatening, humiliating, intimidating, pushing, taking personal belongings, name-calling, making threats, manipulating, and engaging in social exclusion and extortion.

Bullying is most destructive when:

- Bullies get what they want from their target.
- Bullied kids are afraid to tell.
- Bystanders simply watch, participate, or look away, rather than intervening.
- Adults see the incidents as simply "teasing" and a normal part of adolescent life.

Bullying is not a normal rite of passage. In her book *The Bully, the Bullied and the Bystander: How Teachers and Parents Can Break the Cycle of Violence*, Barbara Coloroso points out that bullying is not about anger or conflict but rather contempt. Most bullies have a powerful feeling of dislike toward others they consider to be worthless, inferior, or undeserving of respect. Bullies intend to hurt emotionally or physically, and they enjoy it.

Bullying cannot be permitted at any level. There needs to be clear rules and policies regarding bullying. Adults need to respond consistently and sensitively to bullying. Parental involvement is essential. Bullied students, bullies, and bystanders all need care. Bullied students need to be encouraged and supported, in ways that acknowledge their strengths and talents. The energy of bullies can be redirected into positive leadership. Bystanders can be taught to stand up, speak out, and act against injustice.

The August 2007 issue of *Pediatrics* reported that those who engaged in frequent bullying were more likely to develop an antisocial personality, substance abuse problems, depression, and anxiety disorders. Those who were bullied were also more likely to develop anxiety disorders. Because childhood bullying is a complex behavior with potentially serious consequences, the early identification of children at risk should be a priority for society.

Today's youth leader must also be concerned with cyber-bullying and harassments via the Internet. Harassment is defined under the law as causing a reasonable person to suffer "substantial emotional distress." The law also prohibits communications by an adult to a child under 18 that would cause a reasonable parent to fear for the child's well-being.

The tragic story of Megan Meier has heightened concern about cyber-bullying and online harassment. In 2006, when she was 13, Megan met a 16-year-old named Josh Evans on the social networking site MySpace. They became close, but suddenly he turned on her, calling her names and saying she was "a bad person" and "everybody hates you." Others joined the harassment—a barrage that culminated on October 16, 2006, when Megan committed suicide, just short of her 14th birthday.

Weeks later, Megan's grieving parents learned that the boy didn't exist—he'd been fabricated by a neighbor, the mother of one of Megan's former friends. Police said the girls had had a falling out, and this parent wanted to know what Megan was saying about her daughter. Local police and the FBI investigated, but no criminal charges have been filed. Megan's mother, Tina Meier, says they have considered a civil suit.

Officials in Megan Meier's hometown outside St. Louis have made online Internet harassment a local crime. It is now a misdemeanor, punishable by a fine of up to $500 and 90 days in jail, to harass someone over the Internet. Tina Meier advises other parents to beware of adults pretending to be kids online. "I'm hoping parents will take an extra step and take a look at their MySpace accounts, their Facebook accounts—it's not just kids. You obviously can have an adult, and it doesn't have to be a sexual predator."

Weapons and Gang Activity

A generation ago, getting accosted by a bully at school or out on the street was the greatest fear of many teens. In recent years, that concern has been folded into the larger specter of violence from gangs and armed students.

A June 2006 statistical report from the U.S. government stated that 18 percent of students had carried a weapon (gun, knife, club) in the last year. Boys were more likely than girls to carry a weapon (30 percent of boys, and 7 percent of girls). The same study showed that 8 percent of students had been threatened or injured by someone carrying a weapon in the previous 12 months. Concerns about the heightened threat of violence have led to schools installing metal detectors at the doors to apprehend students carrying guns, knives, and other weapons.

The rise of gangs is equally frightening, and another challenge for those of us in youth ministry. My friend Brian Smith runs a ministry just outside Reno that has made an effort to minister to a group of kids who refer to themselves as "straight-edge kids." Yet the story Brian shared with me in a recent email shows how difficult it can be to provide a safe atmosphere for all students while reaching out to those involved in gang-like behavior:

Straight edge is composed of, in their own description, bored skinny white kids. They believe in no drinking, no drugs, and sleeping with only one girl at a time. The problem, though, is that if you do any of the things they're against, or if you get on their bad side, they will beat you up. Their method involves many on one or two, so the odds are in their favor.

We had many straight-edge kids showing up initially. We celebrated them coming; however, they were the reason many other kids stopped coming. When they were here on Wednesday nights, they threatened other kids both verbally as well as simply with their presence. We even had an incident where they tried to mace a kid as he drove by in his jeep. Luckily they missed their target. However a report was filed, and the police came by the church to ask me some questions.

At that point the reality that the youth group was not safe for the other kids became very clear. We decided straight edge could no longer make this their place; it had to be a place for all youth in the community. Apparently the straight-edge kids were using our gatherings as a place to connect with other straight-edge kids from different schools and make plans for the future. These plans were not exactly in keeping with God's vision for the youth in our community! We even had a kid 'jumped' just outside our youth room. This was a kid I was discipling too! What a bummer. During one of our services, the kids acted up and drew all sorts of attention to themselves. It was tough to keep them focused. Unfortunately we saw little life change in them.

Luckily, we had a few police officers who were supportive of our youth group and our mission. They were also in support of creating safe environments by diffusing the straight-edge presence. We decided that anyone wearing straight-edge insignias or paraphernalia would be sent home without question. I had to ask a handful of teens to leave because they were claiming straight edge. Of course, this was not well received, and their members gave some extreme resistance. The resistance ended when the cop in plainclothes stepped forward, removed the Velcro patch from his shield, and told the youth to leave the property. Straight edge was no longer tolerated at our church.

The fallout on MySpace that night and the next week was incredible. The names used for me were colorful at best. For a short time following that first encounter with the police, the straight-edge kids continued to come. They were allowed in as long as they didn't show anything straight edge or talk about it. We still had some trouble initially. The police were called two other times before youth group meetings—to prevent a fight posted on MySpace and to respond to an anonymous warning.

Unfortunately we don't see these students around anymore. By themselves they are incredible kids, and most of them love to talk about God and faith. Together though, the mob mentality sets in, and they want to fight anyone that looks cross at them. On several occasions, I've met with a student and his parents to let them know I would like to meet with the young person outside of church with the intent of maintaining some sort of ministry in his life. These offers fell on deaf ears.

Drawing the line with straight edge was a difficult call to make. We celebrated that we had fringe kids in the youth group, but lamented the fact that very few of our 'church' kids wanted to come back to youth group meetings. And if kids came, very few invited their friends. Looking back, I know I made the right decision.

As I write this, my heart breaks for P. R. Sherman. I liked this straight-edge kid. We would meet weekly at Starbucks and talk about what God was teaching him. I saw him begin to open up his Bible and read it. I even spent some time pouring my life into his up on the slopes one winter. I also had the opportunity to help counsel him and his parents. I called him a month ago and haven't heard back from him. He is a stud and well liked by everyone. I just don't know what God has in store for him.

"Honey... they brought him back!"

Alcohol and Substance Abuse Problems

The young person who is recovering (never recovered) from an alcohol or substance abuse problem has usually lived more life than most of us would ever want to see. These kids are both more and less mature than their peers. You'll find them in any youth group—no one church has the monopoly on the "good kids" who don't do drugs or alcohol. Students with substance abuse problems, and those in recovery, have special needs we must recognize and learn about. And in many—if not most—of our communities, there is a crying need for such ministry to be done.

Recent research indicates that as much as 10 percent of the entire United States population is chemically dependent. That's 30 million people, including kids and adults, who are addicted to alcohol, drugs, or both. None of these men and women, boys and girls, can find healing from their addictions on their own. They need treatment and support. In response to growing awareness about the prevalence of alcohol and drug abuse, treatment centers have opened around the country in great numbers.

The National Institute of Alcoholism and Alcohol Abuse found some disturbing results in a recent nationwide study of high school seniors. The study concluded that, in an average class of twenty kids, one drinks alcohol daily, one smokes marijuana daily, one has used cocaine in the last month, and twelve have consumed alcohol in the last month. By the time they graduate from high school, nine of ten kids will have experimented with some mood-altering chemical—alcohol, marijuana, or worse. This behavior often intensifies in college, out of the suspicious gaze of mom, dad, and the church family.

I was encouraged to hear that drug use among teenagers in 2007 was down compared with 2002. But the numbers remain disturbing: 42 percent of high school seniors have used marijuana, and 8.5 percent have tried cocaine. And underage drinking has remained at consistently high levels. The 2005 National Survey on Drug Use and Health estimated there are 11 million underage drinkers in the United States. Nearly 7.2 million are considered binge drinkers (meaning they drink more than five drinks on occasion), and more than two million are classified as heavy drinkers.

In 2007 the U.S. Surgeon General's office issued a national Call to

Action against underage drinking. "Too many Americans consider under-age drinking a rite of passage to adulthood," said acting Surgeon General Kenneth Moritsugu. "Research shows that young people who start drink-ing before the age of 15 are five times more likely to have alcohol-related problems later in life. New research also indicates that alcohol may harm the developing adolescent brain. The availability of this research provides more reasons than ever before for parents and other adults to protect the health and safety of our nation's children."

Let's stop kidding ourselves; many of these kids are in our youth groups, and they are in need of our support, intervention, and long-term help. For a long time we in ministry have stuck our heads in the sand about the matter of addiction, too often dismissing addicts as weak, dis-obedient to God's expressed commands, or simply no good. Perhaps we ought to save the moral judgments for something really worthwhile and focus instead on working with the young people God has given into our care who are trying to make it out of the hell of chemical dependency. If nothing else, a kid may come into our youth group who has begun his recovery, is really searching for Christ in his life, and needs our support rather than our disdain.

Kids in recovery often experience a great void in their lives once the drug that filled their time and gave them meaning is gone. We have a unique opportunity to fill that void with the knowledge and love of God in Jesus Christ. Virtually every recovery program—including both Alco-hol and Narcotics Anonymous—urges the addicted person to hand over his or her life to a Higher Power. Following this, the person must take a fearless moral inventory of what they've done under the control of chemi-cals, seek forgiveness from both God and those hurt by their actions, and move out into life seeking the peace and serenity that God alone can give. That is pretty heavy stuff for the average 16-year-old; but when kids come to grips with these principles, they are making a step toward maturity in Christ their nonaddicted peers may not even comprehend.

How shall we minister most effectively to recovering youth? John Throop suggests four things a youth leader can provide to a youth in recovery:

Presence. After intervention has taken place with a member of your youth group, visit the youth as soon as possible. These kids need your support at this time more than ever. Just being there assures them of your love and care and support. The kids will be carrying around all the guilt they need; once that guilt begins surfacing, you'll be a valuable resource.

Prayer. Pray for your recovering members every day. They need God's help and presence one day at a time. Try to learn exactly where they are in their treatment so your prayer can be targeted. They can fall away from recovery at any time; they remain in recovery by the sheer grace of God. Your prayers do make a difference.

Partnership. As more recovering youth join your group, pair them together for mutual support. Chances are they'll know one another from the AA/NA meetings, but in your youth group you can be much more explicitly spiritual.

Program. As you work with your recovering members, be on the lookout for kids who are at a spiritual point where they can share a testimony of what God has done in their lives. Regardless of the polish of these youths, the other members of your youth group will listen intently because of the integrity of the speaker. These kids can be a real encouragement to your youth group members that it's okay to say no to drugs and alcohol.

It may also be helpful to bring members of your youth group to an open AA/NA meeting. Some meetings allow anyone to come and see what AA/NA is about; other meetings are for members only. In many communities, there is an AA/NA chapter that is made up specifically of teens. If there's an open meeting there, a group can learn a lot by attending.

Your congregation can provide a great service and ministry to the community by housing a teen AA/NA group. Some of your youth group members may well be part of such a meeting. You can also extend a subtle invitation to the participants to come and join your youth group.

The field is fertile with young people coming out of the nightmare of alcohol and drug addiction and into the life of recovery. We must be ready to receive them with the kind of unconditional love shown by the father in Jesus' parable of the prodigal son. Kids in recovery are sadder, wiser, still confused—but most of all, they are sober. They know what it is to be forgiven. Now they need to know from us what it is to be loved.

"Oh no—the first Church youth van just pulled in!" © 1991 Dan Pegoda

Vandalism

Some neighborhood kids had vandalized the church building. They didn't take anything, but they did considerable damage. They painted profane sayings all over the walls, dumped garbage on the floors, smeared human feces in restrooms, and littered the church with empty beer cans.

This kind of malicious damage can sicken and squelch your teens' enthusiasm to reach out to unchurched high-risk kids. They feel discouraged. Why would kids do such a thing—especially to the "house of the Lord"?

When kids vandalize church property and get caught, we have an incredible opportunity to flesh out Christ's love. Teenage vandals typically don't have healthy adult role models, good peer relationships, or good self-concepts. And they have little or no relationship with God or the church. How we respond will speak volumes about what's most important to us.

I don't mean when kids vandalize church property and get caught that we do nothing. We're to be good stewards over all the gifts God gives us. But we need to make sure we're not more concerned about caring for a building than we are about caring for people.

Take Doug Runyon, youth minister from Nashville, Tennessee, for example. He first met Brian when Brian came to the church to apologize for the red spray-painted scribbling on the side of the church building, a bus, and a car's headlights. The police caught Brian in the act and gave him a choice between juvenile court or apologizing and helping with the cleanup. He chose to apologize and help.

"Although a bit skeptical, I invited him along on our all-night outing that evening," says Doug. "He showed up with several friends…That was a year and a half ago. His friends no longer come, but Brian is a regular." The group's love and acceptance kept him coming back.

Not all teenagers apologize for vandalizing a church. But you can find other opportunities to show love and acceptance.

When kids vandalize church property, some youth leaders turn the situation over to the authorities and completely wipe their hands of any further responsibility. Kids who vandalize church property are usually charged with criminal mischief—a misdemeanor in most states—and then a judge assigns a fine, incarceration, or probation, taking into account any prior history with the police and the recommendations of his staff.

But judges are often responsive to a church's suggestion that kids face the consequences of their action by making restitution—making things right—as an option of punishment. Kids can work a certain number of hours to compensate for the damage they do. For example, they may do maintenance, janitorial, or clerical work for the church they vandalize.

View the offense as an opportunity—but recognize that some kids will turn their backs on the church. They may act hostile. Don't let that stop you from trying. Be creative. Brainstorm possible ways to move toward reconciliation with kids who vandalize your church property. Trust the results of your efforts "to him who is able to do immeasurably more than all we ask or imagine, according to his power that is at work within us" (Ephesians 3:20).

You can use a similar approach with students in your group in response to minor incidents of intentional or accidental damage to the church building. Require that students repair, clean up, or pay for the damage they've done—and then some. For instance, if a young person writes on a wall, he should be required to wash all the walls in the room. If a student sticks gum under her chair, she should be required to scrape gum off all the chairs in the room. If a kid breaks a window, he should pay for it. The young person may have to work out a way to pay back any damages. They can be paid back in cash, or the expense for repairs can be worked off—perhaps earning $10 an hour by doing work around the church.

Because every situation is unique, deal with kids on an individual basis. We can respond in different ways. Always start with prayer. And then consider your options. You may decide the problem can be handled adequately by confronting the teenager directly and/or contacting his parents. Or you may decide to alert legal authorities. Pressing charges isn't easy, especially when you pray for and work at restoring relationships with kids. But sometimes it's the most loving thing you can do.

Kids in Legal Trouble

There are a number of practical ways adult youth leaders can help young people (and families of those young people) who have gotten themselves in trouble with the law. Let's begin, however, by considering the major obstacle we youth leaders often face in responding to such situations—we aren't told about the problem.

It's not surprising that many parents choose to remain silent when their son or daughter is in trouble with the law. They may be hoping their child (and the family) will be spared further embarrassment. Others are concerned that their son or daughter will be labeled "troublesome" or "delinquent." Adult youth leaders must continually remind parents—through meetings for parents and teenagers, newsletters, special parenting seminars, and personal relationships—that the youth staff is ready and eager to support them through the bad times as well as the good.

We can assist parents by learning about the juvenile justice system. Most parents have no idea how the courts handle kids. If parents know we have knowledge of the police and court systems, they will be more eager to contact us in a time of need.

Whether a teenager is charged with a relatively minor crime (like shoplifting) or a more serious offense, the legal procedure used by most states and counties follows the same pattern. Generally, when a suspected offender is arrested or brought in for questioning (at police headquarters or a juvenile detention facility), an intake evaluation is completed. This includes gathering information from the arresting officer and the juvenile. In some instances, where no prior police record exists and the crime is relatively minor, a "lecture/release" might be deemed appropriate. The young offender is given a warning and sent home. Otherwise, a probable cause hearing is set to determine whether sufficient evidence exists to justify continuance of the process. If probable cause is established, a trial date is set when the case will be heard before a judge or (in certain situations) a judge and jury. If the judge or jury at the trial decides the evidence proves guilt beyond reasonable doubt, then a disposition hearing is set. At the disposition hearing after weighing all possibilities and recommendations, the judge will rule on what treatment or punitive measures the court will order.

Some offenders will be detained in a juvenile facility throughout this entire process, if the court has reason to believe there are factors that might prevent the juvenile from appearing in the next phase of the process. Many juvenile facilities (short-term detention and long-term treatment) welcome the involvement of clergy or church-related adult youth leaders who desire to maintain a continuing relationship with young parishioners who have been institutionalized. Although some facilities require strict adherence to regular visiting-hour procedures, most will be flexible enough to accommodate a pastor or adult youth leader's schedule.

Rich Van Pelt, in *The Youth Worker's Guide to Helping Teenagers in Crisis*, suggests a few ways to maximize ministry to young people who are incarcerated:

1. Take time to understand the institution's policies, procedures, and activities so you can better understand the young offender's situation. Remember that for most kids, incarceration is a distressing situation, no matter how cynical or calm they appear on the surface.

2. Develop relationships with staff counselors and chaplains within the institution. You'll enjoy even greater freedom when those in charge see you as cooperative, trustworthy, and part of the team.

3. Don't make assumptions about a facility simply because it is county or state operated. Through the years, I've been privileged to work in institutional settings where the rehabilitative atmosphere was excellent. The chaplain's office may already be offering outstanding programs and resources you can support. Above all, recognize that you are not in competition with the institutional staff. Your support of their efforts and their support of yours can really benefit kids.

4. Be aware of manipulative behaviors. The well-meaning but naive adult youth leader can be a prime target for the developing "con" to practice on. In their desperate search for understanding, love, and acceptance, teenagers often manipulate adults for their own ends. They may take advantage of your relationship to earn favor with other staff members. The orientation and training sessions offered by most institutions may help volunteers identify and confront manipulative attempts.

5. Learn to be a deep listener. In institutions, kids are thrust into a suspicious environment. Fearful that anything they say can, may, and probably will be used against them, they often withdraw and allow relationships to be only superficial. Because you represent the "outside world" and because you may have an existing relationship with the inmate from your group, there is greater possibility for more intimate sharing.

6. Keep promises you make and don't make promises you may not be able to keep. If you say you're going to visit on a particular day, make every effort to be there. If you can't, call and make sure the teenager gets your message and your apology. Be consistent and dependable.

7. Leave books, magazines, and electronic music devices (if permissible) with the young person. Kids living in institutions generally have too much free time. They may welcome reading and listening

material. Your youth group may enjoy helping to provide these materials.

8. Be aware of the young person's need for nonsexual physical affection. In relating one-on-one, you can often provide support through appropriate touching and hugging.

9. Be there when he gets out. Reentry is tough. Give a brother a hand.

Now Ask Yourself

1. How would you respond to Randy, Sharon, and Mike mentioned in the beginning of this chapter?

2. What influences teenagers to participate in the kinds of negative and damaging behavior mentioned in this chapter?

3. How do you feel about students who tease other students?

4. If you were Megan Meier's youth leader and learned about the harassment she was experiencing on the Internet, what would you have said or done?

5. How physically and emotionally safe is your youth group? Rate it on a scale of 1-10, with 1 representing very dangerous and 10 meaning extremely safe. Brainstorm how you can make your youth group a community that is physically and emotionally safe.

6. Did Brian make the right choices with the "straight-edge" students? What would you have done differently?

7. How effective is your church in reaching out to kids in your church and community who struggle with alcohol or drugs?

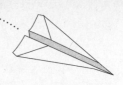

The Challenges of Learning
Differences and AD/HD

There are more than 4.3 million students with learning differences in the United States. And the number is growing. In the last ten years, the number of "special education" students in U.S. schools has increased by 20 percent. Still, the school system overlooks many students with learning differences. And so does the church.

Youth groups subtly ostracize kids with learning differences. Students with learning differences—whether those differences involve emotional struggles or mild mental challenges—make many people feel uncomfortable. Since young people with learning differences are often separated from other youth in school, some kids in our ministries have had very little contact with students with learning challenges. Kids who feel uncomfortable around students with learning differences tend to release their anxiety through unguarded condescension and crude joking. And students with learning differences, because they are often separated from their peers, often have less developed social skills.

Pastor Jude Fouquier believes adult leaders can help their group learn to accept students with learning challenges by modeling that acceptance themselves. Fouquier is the senior associate pastor at The City Church in Kirkland, Washington, and has spent many years as a youth minister at churches in both Missouri and Colorado. In an article that appeared in *Group* magazine, Jude urged youth pastors to take their lead from Jesus—who not only accepted but also sought out people on the fringes. Jesus spent time with epileptics, paralytics, and people suffering from all kinds of diseases (Matthew 4:23-25). Fouquier writes, "When the youth group members see a leader accepting someone—and most of our leaders are cool and someone to look up to—they learn to accept that person."

Just as you can often pick out the brightest kids in your group simply by talking with them, you can often identify students with learning differences when you ask questions, listen, and observe their behavior. The American Academy of Child and Adolescent Psychiatry reports that the following signs could be an indication a student may have a learning difference:

- Trouble understanding the concept of time;
- Difficulty distinguishing right from left—for example, confusing "25" with "52" and "no" with "on";
- Lack of coordination when they walk or play sports;
- Failing schoolwork because of poor reading, writing, or math skills;
- Trouble following instructions;
- Tendency to lose things, such as books; and
- Difficulty remembering what someone has just said.

But students with learning differences are not always easily identifiable. Kathy is a high school cheerleader who attends class regularly and gets average grades. You might never know she had a learning difference. But twice a week a tutor visits her home to help her with reading assignments. When Kathy takes a test that involves a lot of reading, she goes to the counseling office, where her counselor reads the questions to her.

If you are aware that a student has a learning problem, approach the student and his or her parents with sensitivity. Parents usually want to discuss their child's special needs, and they can often teach you how to work most effectively with that student. Jim, for example, will ramble on and on. His parents have learned to stop him by saying, "Jim, that's enough." That may seem abrupt—even rude—to you, but parents often know the best way to respond to their child.

When a Student Is Embarrassed to Read Aloud

Students with learning differences need extra care and sensitivity in a youth group setting. They may fear as they enter your meeting room that they will be embarrassed and humiliated as they've been in school. Make sure these students know they will not be called on to read or answer aloud in front of the group unless they want to be.

Some students with learning differences like to read aloud as long as they have an opportunity to practice. You can allow for this by giving such students the Scripture text ahead of time, so they can be prepared mentally and emotionally. This can be a great way to help such students feel a part of the group. Let them know it is okay to say, "I don't want to today," if they are called on to read and don't feel ready or able.

Several years ago I had a student with learning challenges in my group (we'll call him Bill). I think one of the reasons Bill and I got along so well was because we spent time together outside of class. I would meet him for a Coke at a fast-food restaurant, and we'd go over next week's youth meeting message in a casual manner. Then in class I would ask Bill questions we'd discussed that I knew he'd feel comfortable answering. Bill felt great because he was able to participate and contribute.

If we're not sensitive to the struggles of students with learning differences, we can easily contribute to the pain and alienation they may feel. In *Dare to Discipline*, James Dobson shares the following story of a tenth-grader who walked into his office and announced he was quitting school:

> I asked him why he was quitting and he said, "I have been miserable ever since I was in the first grade. I've felt embarrassed and stupid every year. I've had to stand up and read, but I can't even understand a second grade book. You people have had your last chance to laugh at me. I'm getting out." I had to tell him I didn't blame him for the way he felt; his suffering was our responsibility.

Discovering Gifts and Talents

Try not to focus on "can't dos." It's important to remember that students with learning differences may struggle with certain tasks, but might excel at others. Look for talents and abilities your students with learning differences can offer the group. Find ways to let your kids contribute and feel involved. Ask a kid to help you set up the room for your meeting, or to tag along as you go upstairs to get a projector cart.

When working with students with learning differences, you may need to make certain accommodations. But don't ignore inappropriate behavior. Decide what behavior is acceptable for each individual student given his or her unique situation—and then stick with your decision.

Be sensitive to the needs of your students with learning differences as you design activities. If a young person in your group is dyslexic and you plan an activity that involves reading, have kids work in pairs rather than individually. Pair the dyslexic person with a caring group member. Then have partners trade off reading portions of the assignment if they both feel comfortable doing this. This puts everyone on the same level, and allows the dyslexic person to feel fully included.

If you're planning to play softball and one of your young people has poor motor skills, use a larger-than-normal, mushy ball. This way, everyone will have equal difficulty playing the game because you've introduced a "challenge" that everyone must overcome.

Don't rely on your own abilities alone in working with students with learning differences. Get others to help you. Terry, who's severely challenged, wanted to go to summer camp but couldn't take care of himself there. So Peter, an adult volunteer, offered to help him throughout the camp. Peter gave Terry the attention he needed. And the group enjoyed summer camp together.

If you build community with the students with learning differences in your group, your teenagers will understand Jesus' ministry more fully. After all, every one of us has certain strengths and certain deficiencies. We all have something to contribute, and we all need help from others.

Kids with Attention-Deficit/Hyperactivity Disorder

A 2006 survey by the National Center for Health Statistics reported that 4.5 million kids ages 3-17 have been diagnosed with attention-deficit/hyperactivity disorder, or AD/HD. Boys are more than twice as likely as girls to have AD/HD. AD/HD is the most common behavioral disorder in children and, contrary to past belief, it doesn't disappear with puberty. Instead it manifests itself in very different, and often more dangerous, ways in adolescence than it does in childhood. So chances are you have at least one junior higher or high schooler with AD/HD in your youth group. (We also now know that 60 percent of children with AD/HD carry symptoms well into adulthood, according to Lybi Ma in *Psychology Today*.)

According to the National Resource Center on AD/HD, there are three recognized forms of AD/HD (inattentive, hyperactive-impulsive, and combined). Although some individuals, including many professionals, use the older term ADD (attention deficit disorder) to refer to the form of AD/HD that does not involve hyperactive behavior, the more current terminology for that condition is "AD/HD, predominantly inattentive type." Simply stated, ADD is one of the three recognized forms of AD/HD.

Many doctors believe the different varieties of AD/HD are caused by chemical imbalances in the brain. People with AD/HD have systems that don't function well without a certain neurotransmitter. Most kids with AD/HD are of normal intelligence and are not "bad kids." Strategies like parental counseling, family therapy, cognitive-behavioral therapy, special remediation, and skill training can help kids with various forms of AD/HD. There are also stimulant medications (Ritalin, Concerta, Adderall, Dexedrine, Metadate) and a nonstimulant medication (Strattera) that have been helpful with some varieties of AD/HD.

AD/HD is most often genetic in origin, and the intensity of the symptoms varies from person to person. And there are still many unanswered questions about its causes. Someone with AD/HD may have a short attention span or inability to stay on task, and have problems maintaining concentration and responding quickly. Depending on the form of the disorder, these kids may also talk incessantly, blurt out certain inappropriate words or sentences, or be distractible, squirm, fidget, pick at things, or be impulsive, or hyperactive. It's important to remember that people with AD/HD are not necessarily hyperactive. AD/HD kids may appear irritable, impatient, easily upset, hard to discipline, and hard to please.

Some youth with AD/HD seem unable to organize their time, will perform tasks carelessly, and are often unable to complete assignments on time. Although AD/HD kids have average and sometimes above-average intelligence, they often struggle academically and socially, resulting in poor self-esteem.

Your understanding is crucial to helping an AD/HD kid be successful in your group. Insensitivity or ignorance will only reinforce a kid's low self-esteem. Find out from the parents what types of difficulties their teen experiences. Also find out his or her strengths and abilities. Then build on those strengths. If the kid is a poor reader, avoid calling on him to read aloud. Or, give him prior notice and allow him to prepare. If the kid is hyperactive, ask for his help in some project or make him your assistant. Keep him busy and direct his energy positively.

Make the extra effort necessary to build relationships with your kids who have AD/HD and understand the ways each kid is unique. You could be the one to make a real difference in each young person's life. While many AD/HD kids are accustomed to receiving love, acceptance, and understanding from their families, they don't always expect it or get it from other people.

You may know a kid who you suspect has AD/HD but has never

been diagnosed. Talk to a trained counselor, educator, or doctor about your suspicions. Ask the expert what changes you need to make in a classroom setting to meet this young person's needs.

Let the parents know about your concerns. Encourage them to meet with the expert. Although parents are usually aware of problems with their kids, they may find it very difficult to admit the problems. Be patient. Parents have probably heard complaints for years and may not have known what to do or may deny the problems. AD/HD kids can be draining on their parents and others, but the rewards of accommodating them are worth the time and effort it takes to do so.

Teaching the AD/HD Teen

Marlene LeFever, in *Youthworker Journal,* gives the following practical steps for youth leaders to take in working with kids with attention-deficit/hyperactivity disorder:

- Pray extra hard. Pray for the teens and pray for yourself and other leaders, that you will be able to help the young people, not add to their problems or lack of self-respect.
- Use visual aids, small-group activities, role-playing, and other teaching methods that demand tactile/kinesthetic participation.
- Allow movement and some talking during class. Counselor James Wiegand reports the words of a boy whose treatment was beginning to work: "You know, I used to talk all the time in class. The teacher would tell me to stop. I could for a little bit, but then before I knew it, I was talking again. This is the first time I have been able to stop talking when my teacher asked me to."
- Provide structure while making concessions. For example, a teacher who doesn't mind giving the teen extra time to finish assignments or even extending assignments beyond class time can help an AD/HD child.
- Use a high level of touch. The good teacher will touch the teen appropriately on the back or shoulder and have the ability to bridge the gap between teacher and student.

- Have good eye contact.
- Have AD/HD kids sit close to the front in classroom situations. They will not only hear better but have fewer distractions.
- Keep a good sense of humor.
- Be easygoing. Don't be so rigid and strict that you'll blow up if kids say something completely weird or out of context. Some AD/HD kids may blurt things out without thinking. It's best to flex with the situation without reinforcing what is negative. You might even laugh and say, "Well, this is a little off the wall." That kind of comment doesn't challenge or reprimand the youth for who he is.
- Be more loving than critical to both the teen and the parents. Leaders have the responsibility to talk to parents about a potential problem. Although parents may be hearing the same message from other sources, someone from the church saying the same thing may carry extra weight.
- Look for the good and be generous in positive reinforcement.

The AD/HD Fake

What about the kid who is disruptive, and when you get ready to discipline him, yells out, "You can't discipline me because I have AD/HD!" Is this fake or real?

The diagnosis of some variety of AD/HD is not an excuse or defense for poor behavior. If a kid truly has AD/HD, she usually doesn't broadcast it. Most AD/HD kids already have low self-esteem—why would they want to risk others' ridicule?

If a kid claims his behavior is a direct result of AD/HD, talk to that young person's parents. They may be able to confirm whether they've seen indicators of AD/HD or whether the student has been diagnosed by a psychiatrist. Move from this conversation with a plan of action. Confront a "faker" and explain the truth about the disorder. Tell the faker that while he may get a few laughs for his comments about AD/HD, someone who truly has AD/HD may cringe at his insensitivity and move further away from ever getting needed help.

Now Ask Yourself

1. How does your church react to kids with learning differences?

2. How did Jesus react to persons with differences? How do you think he'd react to your kids?

3. List some ways you could team up with parents of kids with learning differences.

4. What are steps you could take to make sure you don't embarrass these kids?

5. How can these kids become a vital part of the youth group?

6. Are there students in your group who have been diagnosed with AD/HD or who you believe may have this condition? How would you describe their behavior?

7. What things did you learn about these kids in this chapter?

8. List some ways you could team up with parents of AD/HD kids.

9. Which of the suggestions by Marlene LeFever resonated with you?

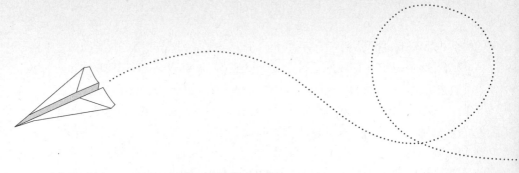

Conclusion

I wrote this book with a prayer that it would be a source of encouragement to those of you who work with challenging youth. I hope *When Church Kids Go Bad* provides you with some practical ideas you can use immediately with your students. And I hope it helps you feel more confident in working with all your kids.

My heart goes out to every one of you who is working with this generation. It's a challenging task, but I am confident God will work through you, just as I've been amazed by the ways God has worked through my own efforts and those who have gone before me.

After 40-plus years of working with young people, I still love them—even the kids who drive me up the wall. And I still believe that loving our kids unconditionally is the most important thing any youth pastor can do. I think Joe Aldrich says it well in Lifestyle Evangelism: "Your church should be the greatest garbage dump in town. A place where the broken, oppressed, misplaced, abandoned, and unloved peoples can come and find a 'family,' where they are accepted and loved…as is. 'As is' people are Jesus' kind of people. The Pharisees despised them. They still do…If your heart is not broken by broken people; you don't have Jesus' heart."

When your kids know that you love and accept them, exactly as they are, they'll be much more inclined to listen to what you have to say and to follow your direction. Love is the greatest motive for obedience. We obey those whom we love. And we love those who first love us (1 John 4:19). When you love and believe in your young people, they'll rise to your expectations.

Of course, your efforts to love your young people won't be perfect. We are all on this journey of life, and none of us has it all together. Mike Yaconelli, in *Messy Spirituality*, wrote, "My life is a mess…For as long as I can remember, I have wanted to be a godly person. Yet when I look at the yesterdays of my life, what I see, mostly, is a broken, irregular path littered with mistakes and failure. I have had temporary successes and isolated moments of closeness to God, but I long for the continuing presence of Jesus." It's true that we're all a bit of a mess. And yet God works in and through messy people just like us. If we continue in our efforts to be faithful, to love our kids as best we can, we'll be surprised by what God can do.

As I conclude this book, I am thinking of Josh Merold. Josh was one of the kids in the youth group at a church I served for 22 years. His grandfather was the senior pastor of the church (my boss). His mother was my secretary. Josh was, to put it mildly, a challenging student to work with. I could fill an entire book with stories of the stuff he got into. While he was in my youth group, I poured a lot of time into Josh and his friends, but there didn't seem to be any change in behavior or attitude.

It wasn't until Josh was a couple of years out of high school that it all came together for him. He wrote me a note apologizing for the pain he had caused. He straightened out his life, went to a Christian college, and is now a senior pastor at a church in California.

My point in telling you that story is to remind you transformation takes time. You may never see the results of your efforts with students this side of heaven. But know that your efforts to share God's love with troubling kids will pay off—you can bank on it. Cling to the promise of Proverbs 22:6: "Start children off on the way they should go, and even when they are old they will not turn from it." Keep doing what you are doing, and know that God will bless your work in ways beyond what you can imagine.

Even when I am old and gray,

do not forsake me, my God,

till I declare your power to the next generation,

your mighty acts to all who are to come.

Psalm 71:18

It's Your Turn: Responding to Youth Workers' Questions

Over the last few years, I've had a number of opportunities to share my ideas on discipline while speaking at youth worker conventions and other gatherings across the country. I often give participants the chance to ask questions about discipline situations they face in their own youth programs. Here's a sampling of some questions I've been asked, along with my responses.

I came into a situation where I was trying to be everybody's friend. Now I want to set down rules. Is it too late?

It's not too late, but it will be difficult to lay down the law at this point. Sit down with your kids and talk about it. Have them help you draw up rules and consequences for breaking them. Mail a copy to the kids and their parents. Remember, if you don't tell them what the consequences are for breaking a rule, it's not fair.

Here's an idea for keeping things light: At the end of a long list of rules, add something funny. Some possible closing lines might include:

- If you don't follow these rules, you will have to wear bell-bottom jeans or a plaid polyester suit with eight-inch lapels (purchased at a thrift store).
- If you violate these rules, you will be tied to a chair in front of a television and forced to watch reruns of *Teletubbies*.
- If you violate these rules, you will have to listen to the complete collected recordings of Billy Ray Cyrus! (Sorry about that, but this list of rules was getting too serious.)

I have a ninth-grader in my group who is constantly talking. He's a smart kid, and I hate to kick him out of the Sunday school class. But right now he is really disruptive. How would you handle this?

First, you have to get the student out of the class when he's being disruptive. Don't embarrass him—you may want to have another adult leader take him out of the class when he starts disrupting. Then you'll need to confront him about his behavior. Let him know the consequences. If he's got leadership potential, you may want to get him personally involved in the class or study by having him teach part of the lesson. Try to let him feel what a teacher goes through!

At our weekly youth group meeting, the kids talk during the announcements. It's hard to control them during this time. Any suggestions?

Try to make the announcements as fast and interesting as possible. Here are a few ideas:

• You could involve the students by dividing them into teams to come up with a creative announcement.
• Dress up in an outlandish costume when giving the announcements.
• Mime the announcement.
• Give the announcements in rap.
• Have a large visual item for each announcement (such as a combination lock for a "lock-in," skis for a "ski trip," a chainsaw for a "service project").
• Use flash paper and set the announcements on fire at the end.
• Make a recording of yourself reading the announcements before your meeting and then play that recording while you are up front attempting to lip sync your own announcements.
• Show a video segment from a familiar movie, but turn off the sound. Have a couple of students offstage who are reading the announcements into a microphone while trying to speak when the actors onscreen speak.
• Tape announcements to candy and throw them out to kids.

- After the announcements, add some kind of break or transition before beginning the next activity.

How do you deal with kids who are disrespectful?

It's important to take time to talk to these students separately. You'll need to affirm that you love them, but that you cannot allow their behavior to go on. You may want to involve a parent. At any rate you can't let the behavior go unconfronted. Choose a nonthreatening environment to talk to the student—such as a fast-food restaurant when it is not busy. Ask, "How can we prevent this from happening again?" Discuss the consequences for future misbehavior.

At retreats I'm always very clear about rules and consequences. When the kids break the rules, I have to follow through with the consequences. But then I feel guilty about having to enforce the rules, and sometimes get repercussions from parents. Often I've backed off because of these feelings. How should I handle this?

Sometimes you just have to live with the guilt. Even when it's difficult, you need to bite the bullet and follow through.

Dealing with angry parents who are upset about how a discipline problem was handled (or how they think it was handled) can be real tricky. Cover yourself. Be sure parents are fully informed of the rules before the retreat. When you have to discipline a young person, you may want to bring another adult volunteer along so a third party can "witness" your actions and help answer a parent's questions later. I know one youth worker who sends out an encouraging letter each year to parents of incoming students. He includes in his letter, "If you promise not to believe everything your teen says happens at youth activities, I'll promise not to believe everything he says happens at home."

I have a group of junior highers who are always kicking and pulling at each other, giving each other noogies, and so on. They also call each other names. How can I get them to cut down on this?

Sometimes a little clowning around is okay, especially when kids have been sitting still for long periods of time. Try to build some of this time into your meetings and have activities that let them "get it out of their systems." But don't allow the students to put each other down with derogatory name-calling. Confront them individually about this behavior.

We have a problem with older kids who drive; they want to run to the store or leave the meeting early. What should I do?

We have a rule stating that students are not allowed to drive to group activities away from the church. Only adults can drive—all the kids have to ride. This rule helps reduce the possibility of accidents and avoids the lack of unity that can result when some kids drive to and from an activity and others ride the church van or bus. In terms of our meeting at the church, we can't stop kids if they want to leave, but we do have a rule that says they can't leave and come back. And if they do leave the meeting, we tell them they need to go home; they can't mill around in the parking lot. You may need to tell the parents if some kids are causing a problem here. Remember to show them you care enough to give those rules.

Do you ever limit the fun, social activities to kids who attend faithfully?

It depends on whether the activity is meant to be an evangelistic outreach or a reward. If it's an outreach event, you should expect non-Christian kids to attend. But I also have events where we do a special activity as a surprise reward after completing some special ministry project we've been doing all year. So we tell our kids that guests may not be invited to this activity. It's okay to reward students as long as you aren't using the reward as a carrot to get kids involved in the first place: You want them to do ministry for its own sake.

Sometimes we have a problem with kids and their music at special events. Do you set any rules about this?

Yes, we have a rule that, on retreats and trips, all personal electronic music devices must be turned off after we arrive at the destination. They can play them on the way up and back, as long as the volume is low enough to not be heard by others. (As you know even with earphones kids sometimes play music so loud you wouldn't know they're using earphones.) One problem with iPods and other electronic devices is that they leave group members too isolated. Sometimes on the way up to a retreat, I encourage kids to leave the devices off for a period of time and enjoy each other's company. On the way back from a retreat, when the kids are tired, we usually let them relax with their music.

I encourage our young people to listen to music by Christian artists. If there's a concern about the type of music they are listening to, I talk to them privately about it. And for the record—the driver always chooses the tunes that are coming out of the sound system in the van.

How do you handle group members who have graduated but want to hang on?

I don't let students switch grades or keep attending after graduation. It's time for them to move into the college-and-career group, even though they may feel like small fish in a big pond. It can be challenging to know how to handle kids who have been kept behind a grade in school. I usually meet with the student and parents to talk about what will work best. Remember that students who are held back in school, though they may be physically more mature than their peers, may be emotionally and psychologically immature.

It's also difficult to know how to handle students who have dropped out of school. I often let them stay with the group they would have been in. After all, they need the help and encouragement. But it can be a challenge for them to obey the rules now that they are "out on their own."

We have a problem with the deadlines for our retreat registrations. It's the parents who don't meet the deadline. What do you suggest?

You want to be consistent in how you handle these things. You need to communicate—actively and in as many ways as possible—with students and parents regarding deadlines (there may be more than one) and cost increases if students sign up late. Always send a letter with a copy of the publicity for the event to the parents, explaining why it's important to have a registration cutoff date. If they don't turn in the registration by the final deadline, the student doesn't go. In some cases, especially where my intended event is evangelistic, I'll add students after the deadline if I'm able. For other activities where an exact count is needed well in advance, I have to stick by my guns. I have sign-up times for three weeks in a row and not just on a single day. I also require that a portion of the cost be paid at the time students sign up. I also have a clear cancellation policy.

What about that age-old problem where you set a time to leave for a retreat or whatever, and kids are late?

Prepare ahead of time for that possibility. I usually take more than one vehicle on an outing and may leave one volunteer driver behind with the smallest vehicle to wait for a few minutes. I also call the student's parents if I know for sure the student was planning on going. I let them know we cannot wait for their student and give them directions to the location if they choose to drive their kid.

Communicate in advance that you will leave on time, and then follow through. You may want to set a time you will meet at the church or elsewhere, without giving the specific time you will leave, giving yourself some leeway for latecomers, loading the buses, etc. On weekend retreats, we don't allow kids to leave the event early, or leave and come back—it disturbs the weekend. In some cases we may arrange for kids to arrive at the event a little later with an adult volunteer or parent, but once kids are there, they stay there.

What would you do about a parent who is volunteering with the group and disciplines his or her child too harshly on an outing? We had a case where, after a couple of warnings, one of our volunteers smacked her daughter in front of everybody. It put a real damper on the mood of everyone, especially the girl.

When parents want to be involved as volunteer leaders, I always try to make sure the student wants his or her parents involved. Sometimes parents have the wrong motives for "helping"—they are overprotective, or want to "spy" on their child, or even are too lenient. When a parent is involved and cracks down too hard on his or her child, I suggest you talk privately to the parent. You should also take time to encourage and affirm the child and help her understand what happened and why it occurred.

I tell parents on youth activities they should not discipline their own kids. This can be a relief to many parents who are also volunteers. I tell them we will take appropriate action, and we'll let them know if we need their assistance. They are to interact with the kids and enjoy being a volunteer leader.

What would you say to a youth leader who tends to be too controlling?

First of all, I'd say that authority and control are important. They are a part of living, and they also have a place in your youth group when used appropriately. The trouble is that control is hard to turn off. The more we use it, the more we want to use it. It's like eating potato chips—once you start, it's hard to stop.

Because control is so easy to use, we may be tempted to use it more often than we should. After all, we may rationalize, an authoritarian approach takes less time, but we can easily get hooked on using control, restraints, and manipulation. Unfortunately, as a result, we no longer come across to our young people as caring and loving adults. As we work with kids over time, I think the goal should be to exert less and less control and become more and more of a positive influence. When we are too tired, too busy, too hurried—at times like these, we can make serious mistakes.

We have a problem with kids talking when others are talking, and then saying "shut up" to each other. How do I put a stop to this?

Talk to each group member separately about the problem. Explain that you won't allow them to put each other down by telling each other to shut up. We want kids to exert positive peer pressure in ways that encourage others to behave, but this must be done in a respectful way.

What do you mean by "positive peer pressure?"

That's where you allow the kids to participate in making the rules and do some policing of their peers. Again, you want to be developing self-discipline—the kind of discipline that comes from within. Be careful of overusing extrinsic motivation like punishments and rewards. Extrinsic motivation works better with kids younger than junior high age.

One of my students has a parent who is very hard on him. I know that if I discipline this student for a problem, his father is likely to punish him even more severely. What should I do?

Whatever problem the student may cause, don't paint it too bleakly to this type of parent. Establish good communication with the parent—keeping him informed of both good and bad behavior. You may feel it's wise to allow the student a second chance before going to the parent, but don't wait too long. If the parent hears of the misbehavior through the grapevine, he could be extra hard on the child. When you are planning to talk to the parent, inform the child so he has some time to prepare the parent for your call. If there are any signs of sexual or physical abuse by the parent, this has to be reported to the authorities.

What kind of discipline would work best with my group, which has many unchurched kids?

Try to be sensitive to individual needs. Do what you can to know and talk to parents, and discover ways to spend extra time with group members outside of regular meetings. Be aware that these kids may not respond to "Would Jesus want you to do this?" but they may be responsive to positive peer pressure.

You say you love all the kids in your group. How do you love even those kids who are giving you real discipline problems?

It's not always easy, but loving kids is a decision you have to make. And confrontation can be a part of that love—in fact, in some cases it has to be part of it. You can "draw the line" in a way that shows love and concern for kids by supporting discipline with positive relationships.

Bibliography

Alexander-Roberts, Colleen. *ADHD and Teens: Proven Techniques for Handling Emotional, Academic, and Behavioral Problems.* Dallas: Taylor Publishing Company, 1995.

Bennis, Warren. "The Unconscious Conspiracy: Why Leaders Can't Lead," from *In Search of Excellence*, eds. Thomas J. Peters and Robert H. Walterman Jr. New York: Harper and Row, 1982.

Benson, Dennis C., and Bill Wolfe. *The Basic Encyclopedia of Youth Ministry.* Loveland, CO: Group Books, 1981.

Berkowitz, Leonard. *The Development of Motives and Values in the Child.* New York: Basic Books, 1964.

Bluestein, Jane, PhD. *Parents, Teens and Boundaries: How to Draw the Line.* Deerfield Beach, FL: Health Communications, Inc., 1993.

Bradley, Michael J. *Yes, Your Teen Is Crazy! Loving Your Kid Without Losing Your Mind.* Gig Harbor, WA: Harbor Press, 2002.

Cannon, Ann B. *Day-to-Day Discipline That Works with Teenagers.* Loveland, CO: Group Publishing, 1990.

Carter, Wm. Lee, Dr. *The Angry Teenager: Why Teens Get So Angry, and How Parents Can Help Them Grow through It.* Nashville: Thomas Nelson Publishers, 1995.

Case, Steven L. *Road Rules: Hundreds of Ideas, Games, and Devotions for Less-Annoying Youth Group Travel.* Grand Rapids, MI: Zondervan, 2003.

Charles, C. M. *Building Classroom Discipline*, 8th ed. Boston: Pearson Education, 2005.

Cline, Foster, MD, and Jim Fay. *Parenting Teens with Love and Logic: Preparing Adolescents for Responsible Adulthood.* Colorado Springs: Pinon Press, 1992.

Coloroso, Barbara. *The Bully, the Bullied, and the Bystander: How Teachers and Parents Can Break the Cycle of Violence.* New York: HarperCollins, 2003.

Crisci, Elizabeth. *What Do You Do with Joe?* Cincinnati: Standard Publishing, 1981.

Dobson, James. *The New Dare to Discipline.* Wheaton, IL: Tyndale House, 1996.

Dodson, Fitzhugh. *How to Discipline with Love.* New York: Signet Books, 1978.

Elkind, David. *All Grown Up and No Place to Go.* Reading, MA: Addison-Wesley, 1984.

Gangel, Kenneth O. "Discipline: A Family's Friend or Foe?" in *Parents and Teenagers*, Jay Kesler, ed. Wheaton, IL: Victor, 1984.

Ginott, Haim G. *Between Parent and Teenager.* New York: Avon Publishers, 1969.

Gluck, Beth, and Joel Rosenfeld, eds. *How to Survive Your Teenager: by Hundreds of Still-Sane Parents Who Did.* Atlanta: Hundreds of Heads Books, 2005.

Gordon, Jeenie. *Turbulent Teens of Panicking Parents.* Grand Rapids, MI: Fleming H. Revell, 1997.

Hauck, Paul. *How to Do What You Want to Do: The Art of Self-Discipline.* Philadelphia: Westminster, 1976.

Hendricks, Howard. *Heaven Help the Home.* Wheaton, IL: Victor, 1973.

Ingersoll, Barbara. *Your Hyperactive Child.* New York: Doubleday, 1988.

Kelly, Kate. *The Complete Idiot's Guide to Parenting a Teenager.* Indianapolis: Alpha Books, 1996.

Kesler, Jay. *Emotionally Healthy Teenagers: Guide Your Teens to Successful Independent Adulthood.* Nashville: Word Publishing, 1998.

———— and Ben Sharpton. *When Kids Are Apathetic.* Elgin, IL: David C. Cook, 1991.

Kolodny, Robert C. *How to Survive Your Adolescent's Adolescence.* Boston: Little Brown and Company, 1984.

Larson, Scott. *At Risk: Bringing Hope to Hurting Teenagers*. Loveland, CO: Group, 1999.

Larson, Scott. *When Teens Stray: Parenting for the Long Haul*. Ann Arbor, MI: Servant Publications, 2002.

Leshan, Eda. *When Your Child Drives You Crazy*. New York: St. Martin's Press, 1985.

MacDonald, Gordon, "The Difference between Discipline and Punishment," in *Parents and Teenagers*, Jay Kesler, ed. Wheaton, IL: Victor, 1984.

Martin, Grant. *The Hyperactive Child*. Wheaton, IL: Victor, 1992.

Maxym, Carol, PhD, and Leslie B. York, MA. *Teens in Turmoil: A Path to Change Parents, Adolescents, and Their Families*. New York: Penguin, 2000.

McPherson, Miles. *Parenting the Wild Child: Hope and Help for Desperate Parents*. Minneapolis: Bethany House, 2000.

Nelson, Jane, EdD, and Lynn Lott, MA. *Positive Discipline for Teenagers: Empowering Your Teen through Kind and Firm Parenting*, 2nd ed. Roseville, CA: Prima Publishing, 2000.

Ma, Lybi. "ADHD: Always on the Go," March 28, 2007, http://psychologytoday.com/articles/pto-20070328-000001.html.

Narramore, Bruce. *Help! I'm a Parent*. Grand Rapids, MI: Zondervan, 1972.

Olson, G. Keith. *Counseling Teenagers*. Loveland, CO: Group Books, 1984.

Paul, Henry, MD. *Is My Teenager OK?: A Parent's All-in-One Guide to the Emotional Problems of Today's Teens*. New York: Kensington Publishing, 2004.

Penner, Marv. *Help! My Kids Are Hurting: A Survival Guide to Working with Students in Pain*. Grand Rapids, MI: Zondervan, 2005.

Plant, J. S. quoted in Norma E. Cutts, *Better Home Discipline*. New York: Appleton-Century-Crofts Inc, 1952.

Pollard, Nick, and Eric Stanford. *Why Do They Do That?: Practical Advice to Parents on How to Tackle Teen Behavior*. Colorado Springs, CO: Lion Publishing, 1999.

Rice, Wayne. *Junior High Ministry* (Revised). Grand Rapids, MI: Zondervan, 1998.

Silver, Larry. *The Misunderstood Child*, 2nd ed. Blue Ridge Summit, PA: TAB Books, 1991.

Sorensen, Kathleen M. *Setting Boundaries with Youth: How to Discipline with Understanding*. Nashville: Abingdon, 1998.

Spotts, Dwight, and David Veerman. *Reaching Out to Troubled Youth*, rev. ed. Wheaton, IL: Victor, 1994.

Strack, Jay. *Good Kids Who Do Bad Things*. Dallas: Word Publishing, 1993.

Strauch, Barbara. *The Primal Teen: What the New Discoveries about the Teenage Brain Tell Us about Our Kids*. New York: Anchor Books, 2003.

Szalavitz, Maia. *Help at Any Cost: How the Troubled-Teen Industry Cons Parents and Hurts Kids*. New York: Riverhead Books, 2006.

Townsend, John, Dr. *Boundaries with Teens: When to Say Yes, How to Say No*. Grand Rapids, MI: Zondervan, 2006.

Tyrrell, Ronald W., Fredrick Hanoch McCarty, and Frank A. Johns. *Growing Pains in the Classroom*. Reston, VA: Reston Publishing, 1977.

Van Pelt, Rich, and Jim Hancock. *The Youth Worker's Guide to Helping Teenagers in Crisis*. Grand Rapids, MI: Zondervan, 2005.

Walsh, David, PhD. *Why Do They Act That Way? A Survival Guide to the Adolescent Brain for You and Your Teen*. New York: Free Press, 2004.

Wiersbe, Warren, "Be Disciplined," in *Parents and Teenagers*, Jay Kesler, ed. Wheaton, IL: Victor, 1984.

Wender, Paul. *The Hyperactive Child, Adolescent, and Adult: Attention Deficit Disorder through the Lifespan*. New York: Oxford, 1987.

Wolf, Anthony E., PhD. *Get Out of My Life but First Could You Drive Me and Cheryl to the Mall? A Parent's Guide to the New Teenager*. New York: Noonday Press, 1991.

Student Life Devotional Series

The Old Testament is full of characters. Spend 48 weeks looking more closely at those characters, and discover more about the character of the God who created us to be part of his story. With daily scripture and thoughts, questions to get you thinking, and plenty of space for you to journal your thoughts, you'll better understand how you fit into the story.

Character
Old Testament People, Encounters with God
Richard Parker
RETAIL $12.99
ISBN 978-0-310-27906-8

Jesus is one of the best-known people in history. But do you really know him? Spend 48 weeks looking at the life of Jesus and discover how he can impact your life. With daily scripture and thoughts, questions to get you thinking, and plenty of space for you to journal your thoughts, you'll get to know the real Jesus, and how you can become more like him.

Christ
The Life of Christ, The Basics of Life
Dr. Johnny Derouen
RETAIL $12.99
ISBN 978-0-310-27905-1

The Church started more than 2,000 years ago, but it still has relevance to us today. Spend 48 weeks looking more closely at the community of the Church. With daily scripture and thoughts, questions to get you thinking, and plenty of space for you to journal your thoughts, you'll find that the Church is more than a building—it's a family.

Community
The New Testament Church, The Essence of Fellowship
Adam Robinson
RETAIL $12.99
ISBN 978-0-310-27907-5

Sacred Space provides dozens of ideas to help students engage in scripture and apply the lesson to their own lives. You'll find step-by-step instructions to create the space and experience necessary to draw your students into the scripture. Through art, listening, writing, and multi-sensory prayer stations, your students will experience God's Word in a whole new way. Includes step-by-step, downloadable PDFs on CD-ROM.

Sacred Space
A Hands-on Guide to Creating Multisensory Worship Experiences for Youth Ministry
Dan Kimball & Lilly Lewin
RETAIL $29.99
ISBN 978-0-310-27111-6

visit www.youthspecialties.com/store
or your local Christian bookstore

youth specialties

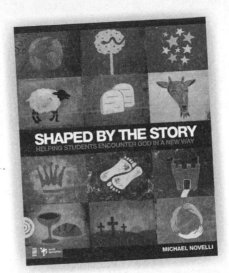

Through the art of "Storying," your students will experience God in a new way. This unique, dialogue-centered approach will spark imaginations and inspire your group to find themselves in God's amazing story. Includes sample narratives and an interactive training DVD.

Shaped by the Story
Helping Students Encounter God in a New Way
Mike Novelli
RETAIL $29.99
ISBN 978-0-310-27366-0

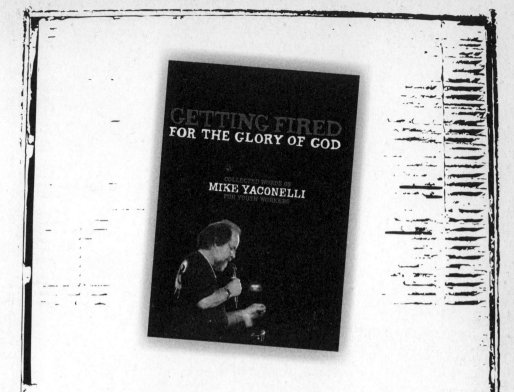

Years after his death, Christians across the world turn to the words of Mike Yaconelli to uncover the divine mischief, the shameless truth-telling, the love of kids, and the passion for Jesus that make youth ministry an irresistible calling. A DVD containing video and MP3 audio speeches is included.

Getting Fired for the Glory of God
Mike Yaconelli
RETAIL $16.99
ISBN 978-0-310-28358-4

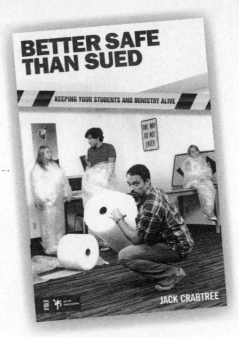